SURVIVAL THEMES IN FICTION FOR CHILDREN AND YOUNG PEOPLE

Second Edition

by
BINNIE TATE WILKIN

Foreword by
Virginia A. Walter

The Scarecrow Press, Inc.
Metuchen, N.J., & London
1993

First edition of *Survival Themes in Fiction for Children and Young People*, by Binnie Tate Wilkin, was published by Scarecrow Press, Inc., in 1978.

British Library Cataloguing-in-Publication data available

Library of Congress Cataloging-in-Publication Data

Wilkin, Binnie Tate, 1933–
   Survival themes in fiction for children and young
people / by Binnie Tate Wilkin. — 2nd ed. / foreword by
Virginia A. Walter.
        p.   cm.
   Includes indexes.
   ISBN 0-8108-2676-3 (acid-free paper)
   1. Children's literature—Bibliography.   2. Children's lit-
erature—History and criticism.   I. Title.
Z1037.W67   1993
011.62—dc20   93-26421

TABLE OF CONTENTS

FOREWORD TO THE SECOND EDITION

When we think about survival themes in children's literature, the books that usually come to mind first are those in which a child's physical survival is in question, where the young protagonist must marshal unexpected reserves of courage, resourcefulness, and endurance. We remember Julie, lost on the Arctic ice fields with only the wolves for companions.[1] And Brian Robeson, first landing a single-engine plane in the Canadian wilderness and then using his only tool, a hatchet, to provide himself with food, clothing, and shelter.[2] Or eleven-year-old Alex, hiding from the Nazis in the abandoned buildings of the Warsaw Ghetto, kept alive by his own ingenuity and his faith that his father will return to find him.[3] Encountering these literary heroes, many young readers find that their own struggles to survive their everyday trials are not so unbearable. Others find it helpful while shaping their own identities to try on those hero roles for size and ask themselves, Could I measure up? What would I do in that situation?

It is the questioning that Binnie Tate Wilkin finds important. She has sought out books for children and young adults that will shake them out of their acceptance of everyday existence and force them to ask questions. The subtext here is that learning to ask the right questions may be the critical survival skill for this generation of young people. We adults have left them with very few viable answers, after all.

The books in this bibliography fall into several broad categories: loneliness, feelings, images of self and others, sexuality, friendship, social interaction, families, the environment, religion and politics, war and peace, life and death. Their intended readers range in age from preschool to high school. Most were published in the 1980s, a decade that saw social and political support for children and youth decline dramatically. Sylvia Ann Hewlett documents this decline on many fronts. The sheer number of children living in poverty increased dramatically during this period, going from 16 percent of all children in 1979 to 23 percent in 1988.[4] While poor children are most at risk of not reaching their full potential, she points out that mainstream children have also been neglected and are more likely than previous generations to underachieve in school, commit suicide, take drugs, get pregnant, or be victims of violent crimes.[5]

This is a generation of children with a shocking firsthand exposure to violence. James Garbarino and his associates at the Erikson Institute in Chicago have documented the trauma of childhood in wartorn Cambodia, Mozambique, Nicaragua, the West Bank—and southside Chicago.[6] A recent article in the *Journal of the American Medical Association* called attention to the crisis of violence in the United States and the effects of this violence on children who witness it. The authors cited studies showing that one out of ten children attending the Boston City Hospital pediatric clinic had seen a shooting or stabbing before they were six years old. Over 90 percent of the children in a New Orleans study had witnessed violence; 40 percent of them had seen a dead body. Between 10 percent and 20 percent of the homicides committed in Los Angeles are witnessed by children.[7] These are scary times in which to be a kid.

Binnie Tate Wilkin has played many roles in the library community. She has been a frontline librarian, providing outreach services to inner-city children in Los Angeles. She has been a lecturer in three different library schools. She has been a library administrator, trainer, and consultant. Concern for children and youth has been the unifying thread in her varied career.

In this bibliography, she provides other professionals who work with children and young people with resources that will give this generation something better than pat answers. These books will help children develop the questions that they must resolve in order to survive as citizens in the twenty-first century.

Virginia A. Walter
Graduate School of Library and Information Science
University of California, Los Angeles

NOTES

1. George, Jean, *Julie of the Wolves*. New York: Harper & Row, 1972.
2. Paulsen, Gary, *Hatchet*. New York: Bradbury, 1987.
3. Orlev, Uri, *The Island on Bird Street*. Boston: Houghton Mifflin, 1984.

4. Hewlett, Sylvia Ann, *When the Bough Breaks: The Cost of Neglecting Our Children.* New York: Basic, 1991, pp. 35–36.
5. Ibid., p. 65.
6. Garbarino, James, Kathleen Kostelny, and Nancy Dubrow, *No Place to Be a Child: Growing Up in a War Zone.* Lexington, MA: Lexington, 1991.
7. Groves, Betsy McAlister, et al. "Silent Victims: Children Who Witness Violence," *Journal of the American Medical Association,* vol. 269, no. 2 (January 13, 1993), pp. 262–264.

FOREWORD TO THE FIRST EDITION

The survival of children in an uncertain world is the name of the game for Binnie Tate Wilkin and she exerts considerable expertise in helping them discover and exploit their life space. When she was on the staff of the Los Angeles Public Library a leadership syndrome gravitated toward her because her colleagues often waited to check out her opinion on a book or a program. She did not seek to be in the forefront but at the same time she spoke with pragmatic elegance on the issues that have changed children's literature from stories about the trip to Grandma's farm to a narrative loaded with pain and despair. The new attitudes in fiction did not always set well with librarians who believed that children should be protected from harsh realities however vicarious, and book selection lines in the library were on occasion taut with tension.

Leadership does not always require overt action. Her positions on books and services, particularly for the inner city and barrio, brought, as she has said, "A number of people to my corner." It would be incorrect to assume that her career has been narrowly conceived. The entire community of children and young people is her bailiwick, with special emphasis on selection and services. She understands the common denominator of childhood that insists upon directness and honesty without equivocation. For Ms. Wilkin, the story is a primary concern.

She became a Senior Children's Librarian in the Los Angeles Public Library in a federally funded project. Working with nine branches in the central region, she assessed community needs, worked with parents, programmed children's services, and assisted children with remedial reading problems. Her "Bookbagger" program distributed free paperbacks to the children. The project "A is for Africa" was a heritage experiment that preceded *Roots* by a few years. Several thousand children and adults have seen her interpretation of African folktales through narration, music, and dance.

The Los Angeles experience was broadened through workshops on inner-city services for various Library Association meet-

ix

ings. This led to writing, and articles in *Library Journal, Interracial Books for Children Bulletin,* and the anthology *Advances in Librarianship* documented her professional work.

In 1970 she joined the University of Wisconsin Library School for two years, training minority librarians as community specialists. This led to a specific interest in teaching and when she returned to California she taught courses on Children's Literature, Book Selection and Inner-City Services at the library school of California State University, Fullerton. In 1976 she became a Lecturer in the Graduate School of Library and Information Science, UCLA, and taught Children's Libraries, Children's Literature, and Library Services for Youth.

Among her ideas about books for children she believes that a realistic presentation of human existence will help them develop their own capabilities in problem solving. The books she selects are intended as samples that offer certain sensitivity to some of the individual and societal issues of the day. The choices include a wide swath of basic children's books extending to the 1970s. Some of the issues are friendship, aloneness, feelings, sexuality, identification, and self-image. Picture books make up some of the selections. She prefers challenging and provocative issues as background for her perceptive and straightforward comments. The selections indicate a belief that books will help young people achieve a sense of values through an awareness of self and environment.

JEROME CUSHMAN
Senior Lecturer
Literature for Children and Adolescents
Department of English
University of California, Los Angeles

INTRODUCTION

About modern children's literature, Rebecca Lukens writes, "Now fortunately for us all there are again available for children as well as adults both the new and old stories and poems that concern the human spirit—its joys and playfulness, its yearnings and triumphs, its sorrows and despairs, every variety of human relationship, every kind of personal search for independence."[1] It is the purpose of this volume to examine contemporary, realistic, children's fiction for examples of writings which explore such issues of human existence and survival. Here, children's materials are considered for the usual elements of good writing but emphasis is placed on the following: a. portrayals of characters which show realistic introspection and growth; b. coverage of social development and interaction; c. depictions of varied personality types and cultures; and d. perspectives of historical, political, and environmental issues. The assumption prevailing is that literature can be enjoyed and at the same time challenge and influence young readers.

In the first edition of SURVIVAL THEMES IN FICTION FOR CHILDREN AND YOUNG PEOPLE, trends in publishing for children were outlined. Substantial evidence supported the theory that children's books, like all other literature, reflect the issues and mores of the times in which they are published. Materials published in the past decade continue to contemplate social and historical developments. Public awareness of such issues as child abuse, incest, and other family problems is reflected in many titles. AIDS as a medical and social problem has emerged, however, growing conservatism probably has thwarted inclinations to deal openly with other elements of sexuality. For a time, an appreciation of rural and farm life was prominent in major commercial films and other media. Likewise, some outstanding titles for children have also appeared with rural or farm settings, and plots with religious emphasis seem more plentiful. While books reflecting purely political issues are few, preserving the environment appears as a concern.

An article titled, "Taking a Look Backward, Newbery Winners Reflect Societal Trends," by Jennifer A. Newton[2], examined Newbery Medal winners from 1951 to 1985 to, "detect trends and

1

changes" during those thirty five years. According to her study, children's books published during this period were, "typically fiction stories with happy endings about white middle-class, twelve to fifteen year olds who live in the rural United States in the second half of the twentieth century." Themes included growing up, family relationships, and crises of family members. Ninety one percent of the books were by white authors. The study included a search for indicators of literary factors which publishers and authors felt were appropriate in writing for children, concluding that idealism played a significant role, as well as presentation of characters to whom children are able to relate. The author notes that it was only after SOUNDER was published in 1970 and was awarded the Newbery Medal that publishers began to seek Black, Hispanic, Asian, and Native American authors. After this, Newton stated, "taboos on homosexuality, drug addiction, unwed mothers, explicit sex, rape and prostitution were relaxed to a certain degree, but still the industry received pressure from conservatives to censor sex, violence, and language." Newton emphasized that the Newbery selections, "generally skirted these sensitive areas." With this study, the discussion continues on what should be written for children, what they are really interested in reading and how much they understand about the issues presented in books written for them.

Assuming the theories of modern child psychologists such as Piaget are correct, the youngest readers are generally unable to make interactive connections for problem solving, but, they are actively involved in experiencing and learning language. Books can add to that learning process. The worst of children's fiction is often that in which authors struggle to present a set of words or to use limited language. Such presentations, lacking exceptional skill, are often flat and emotionally numb. Even the most primary children's fiction can provide language which is alive, and which allows readers to celebrate life on their own terms. Moreover, through the sharing of literature, seeds of information and images of life are being rooted for the young child's future analysis.

Children in the early to middle grades of elementary school are in, what Piaget terms, the "operational" stage of development. They may sometimes be more absorbed in their own ability to read, than in what the story accomplishes. As Max Luthi says about children experiencing fairy tales, "The image of man portrayed in the fairy tale—or, rather, one aspect of this image—is that of one who has the capability to rise above himself . . . We can be sure that children, engrossed in the story as it is told to them, do not understand this in all its implications, but, what is more important, they sense it."[3] The response to realistic fiction may be much the same. Children will *sense* many things about characters which they will not be able to rationalize. They are, absorbed with language, images, values, etc. which become the basis for questioning soon to begin. Although younger children may not be obsessed with their personal identity, they are busily identifying what it means to be a human child in an adult ruled world. Many fiction books for the middle years, accurately deal with learning the rules.

Generally, it is agreed that adolescents are ready for all ingredients in their literature. They have begun the process of questioning, making relationships, and seeking answers. They are preparing themselves for the not too distant and sometimes frightening trip into adulthood. In his ARBUTHNOT HONOR LECTURE, Aidan Chambers spoke about the adolescent novel, referring to the works of Robert Cormier, Paul Zindel, Louise Fitzhugh, and Mildred Taylor as being like Huckleberry Finn in their presentation of adolescent truths. "The central concern of adolescence, therefore, is freedom to be," he said. In regard to his own novels, BREAKTIME and DANCE ON MY GRAVE, Chambers asked, "How do we invent ourselves and what does it feel like?" These questions, he proposed, forced him to deal with what he called "matters of the spirit."[4] Throughout this volume, emphasis has been placed on such matters of the spirit. "Survival" applies to those books which provide characters who struggle with matters of heart and circumstance, and who are involved in experiences which challenge young people to question. Seeking answers may be the most important exercise of childhood and adolescence. Books of fiction need not provide all the answers, but the best books directed to youth may provide the questions. Readers draw personal conclusions from the evidence rather than from the answers. That evidence is provided through good characters, humanized to expose their sensitivity to the setting and situation in which they are placed. In this regard, many children's books fail, since, unlike the adult novel, numerous titles represent "slices of life" allowing the child reader a limited view of the complexities of human nature.

For the issues dealt with, some of such "slice of life" stories are included here. The best of these present an issue through the natural delineation of the character, perhaps even as an afterthought. Interaction between some characters may be forceful enough to forgive other characters which are cardboard or flat.

Selections for this volume were made primarily from books published in the last decade. Some inclusions published in the late seventies and early eighties are now out of print, but are still available in many libraries. Materials have been categorized in sections and chapters as follows:

THE INDIVIDUAL
    Aloneness and Loneliness
    Feelings
    Individual Growth and Development
    Sexuality
PAIRINGS AND GROUPINGS
    Friendship; Peer Pressures; Social Interaction
    Families
VIEWS OF THE WORLD
    People and the Environment
    Religion and Politics
    War and Peace
    Celebration of Life and Death

Books have been roughly categorized as: Youngest (pre-school); Younger (early school years); Middle (middle elementary to upper); Older (upper elementary to junior high); and Oldest (junior high and up). At the end of each section, PROGRAM-MING SUGGESTIONS are given. The ideas are purposefully general, so that parents, teachers, librarians, and others can vary them as necessary.

SOURCES AND NOTES are presented in the last section. These notes include sources for additional information on the titles reviewed, and for titles reviewed by others which align with the designated categories. Some sources illuminate aspects of children's lives and needs in relation to literature. Since there was no attempt to be all inclusive, this section is important for those who wish to expand on the titles offered here. (It should also be noted that many titles and sources listed in the first edition of SURVIVAL THEMES . . . are still available.) References for additional programming information are also included.

NOTES

1. Lukens, Rebecca, "What Literature Can Do For Children," in *Anthology of Children's Literature* by Zena Sutherland and Myra Cohn Livingston. Glenview, Ill.: Scott Foresman & Co., © 1984.

2. Newton, Jennifer A., "Taking A Look Backward, Newbery Winners Reflect Societal Trends," in *Top of the News,* vol. 43, no. 1 (Fall, 1986), pp. 97-102.
3. Luthi, Max, *Once Upon a Time.* Introduction by Francis Lee Utley. New York: Frederick Ungar, © 1970, p. 140.
4. Chambers, Aidan, "All of a Tremble to See His Danger." May Hill Arbuthnot Lecture, in *Top of the News,* vol. 42, no. 4 (Summer, 1986), pp. 405-423.

SECTION I
THE INDIVIDUAL

Aloneness and Loneliness
Feelings
Individual Growth and Development
Sexuality

I. THE INDIVIDUAL

Aloneness and Loneliness

Many novels for children and young people center on one or more aspects of growth and maturation. The focus is often on social development rather than on the emotional growth of the individual, although emotional growth may be suggested. Some titles use aloneness or loneliness as a tool for the story's development or resolution. For example, loners, as characters in children's books, frequently develop an acceptance of their individual differences. The protagonist may be one who uses moments alone to pursue special interests, to write, or to take measures for self improvement. Other loners suffer from psychological isolation felt even when in the company of others. These characters, more often than not, are facing some crisis in their lives, or, are having problems living up to social "norms." Loneliness may be used by an author to present a condition from which a character can rise above the odds. Commonly, child characters, alone, are faced with decision making which ordinarily would be perceived of as beyond their capacity.

Crucial in adolescent development is the fact that loneliness can become pathological or promote pathological reactions, especially when coupled with low feelings of self worth. Some stories examine these emotional extremes. In contrast, aloneness may be a temporary feeling of isolation. Creative use of time can temper such feelings. In a few titles, the individual realizes that choices about aloneness are their own. Books for very young children often portray the natural adjustment to aloneness through imaginary play. Loneliness can be the product of numerous circumstances, and such circumstances provide the background for some of the more interesting children's novels.

BEHIND THE ATTIC WALL by Sylvia Cassedy. New York: Thomas Y. Crowell, 1983. Middle-Older

Margaret Ann Turner, an orphan, has been sent to live in a very big house with her great aunts. After living in group homes, Margaret anticipates that life with her elderly relatives will not be pleasant. Little does she know that the big house is a former school for girls and that the aunts are sticklers for manners and decorum. Although the elderly women mean well, they have few sensibilities about raising a young child.

With this setting, the stage is set for the main character's difficult life ahead. For Margaret, the only moments of relief from a very strict life will be found with humorous Uncle Morris, at play in the immense garden behind the home-school, and with the dolls which she discovers in the attic.

While seeking protection from the real world of wearing dull brown uniforms to school, being laughed at, and having no friends, the author simultaneously moves Maggie through the transition to a half real–half fantasy life. It starts when she begins to hear voices, and when she discovers the attic dolls, which talk to her. In a somewhat "Alice in Wonderland" atmosphere, which Maggie creates for herself in the attic, tea and conversations are held with the dolls. When at play in the garden, she talks to imaginary playmates. Her previous experiences of loneliness have produced "The Backwoods Girls" illusory playmates to whom Maggie can feel superior.

The author's writing is an intriguing and compelling mix of realism, imaginary play, and fantasy. This fictional child's search for solace is disturbing and unrelieved. In the end she is forced to move on to another unknown place with no promise of what her new situation might be. Within the final pages, even Uncle Morris dies and, during her last visit to the attic, Maggie finds evidence that he has joined the dolls.

This is a haunting, disturbing novel which many readers will explore for its touches with fantasy. Only discussion will reveal what feelings are touched in the reader by this story of a child very much alone.

BLACKBERRIES IN THE DARK by Mavis Jukes. Pictures by Thomas Allen. New York: Alfred A. Knopf, 1985. Younger-Middle

Austin feels lonely and sad when he visits his grandmother after grandpa has died. Talks with grandma and a fishing trip help him conquer loneliness. Soft pencil illustrations add to the mood of the story. Jukes writes "homey" titles for the young including LIKE ME AND JAKE, about a warm relationship between a young boy and his stepfather. (Also use with CELEBRATION OF LIFE AND DEATH)

DAN ALONE by John Rowe Townsend. New York: Lippincott, 1983. Middle-Older

Although the eleven year old boy, portrayed in this Dickens-like story is not alone, his struggle to find balance in his life is a lonely one. Complex turns of events, deftly delineated in the first passages of the book, leave Dan with the knowledge that the man he has thought was his father is not, and that his real father might be alive. His mother is involved in an affair with a married man and leaves Dan to live with his strict and opinionated grandfather. When his grandfather becomes ill, the boy is sent to live with an Aunt, who doesn't want him. Dan then runs away seeking his father, whom he has been led to believe may be wealthy.

The search places Dan in circumstances which summon all of his instincts for survival. While hiding out, he forms an alliance with a young girl who is retreating from her child-beating surrogate father. Later, Dan becomes associated with a family of thieves. They encourage him to beg and sing for money outside of local pubs.

In the background is Benjy, a kind man, rejected and referred to with racial epithets because he is Jewish. (Earlier in the story, it has been established that Dan's grandfather hates Jews and Catholics.) Benjy is Dan's real father.

After several frightening adventures, Dan returns to his aunt, but continues in his search for the truth. After learning that his mother is no longer with the married man, Dan finds her and arranges a reunion with Benjy—but all is not well—Benjy is ill and hostile members of the family undoubtedly will not accept him. Dan, however, has found what he wanted, a real family.

Some elements of the story, upon examination, are not believable, but the author provides a variety of ingredients and characters. The resulting adventure and excitement will delight many readers.

THE DO-SOMETHING DAY by Joe Lasker. Illus. by author. New York: Viking, 1982. Youngest

Feeling alone because he can't get anyone's attention, Bernie runs away. The old-fashioned illustrations add a special flavor.

FRITZ AND THE BEAUTIFUL HORSES by Jan Brett. Illus. by the author. New York: Houghton Mifflin, 1981. Younger

A pony is used to show loneliness to the very young. The pony named Fritz is lonely because he is separated from the other horses. In the end, Fritz emerges as a hero.

THE ISLAND ON BIRD STREET by Uri Orlev. Translated by Hillel Halkin. New York: Houghton Mifflin, 1984. Middle-Older

Peripheral to this title are the war and the horrors of the holocaust, but the story presents an example of isolation and loneliness. Alex, the main character, hides out in the basement of a house, awaiting the return of his father and hoping the Nazis will not discover he is there. For weeks and months he is alone except for his pet mouse. This circumstance plus those moments when he ventures from the house to find food and other survival supplies, provide the necessary suspense to sustain the story.

Some of the feats which Alex is able to accomplish seem unrealistic, although, time after time stories document the unusual resiliency and resourcefulness of children found in such circumstances. Vivid descriptive scenes of Poland and the ruins of war are given. The story is designed as a tribute to the many who suffered through and survived similar situations, as well as to those who died. (Also use with books on WAR AND PEACE)

JACOB AND OWL: A STORY by Ada Graham and Frank Graham. Illus. by Frank and Dorothea Stoke. New York: Coward, 1981. Younger-Middle

Nursing an injured barn owl helps Jacob fill his moments of aloneness, after his parents have separated.

JULIE'S TREE by Mary Calhoun. New York: Harper and Row, 1988. Middle

Julie has just moved to a new town and is too shy to make friends. She finds a tree in the middle of town which she climbs daily and from which she watches the passersby. It is here that Julie meets her first friend.

Later, when the tree is slated for removal to allow for developers, Julie leads a "Save the Tree" movement.

This is a slight but sometimes humorous story showing the young how loneliness can be eradicated by involvement. The book could also be used to support environmental studies.

LONESOME LESTER by Ida Luttrell. Illus. Megan Lloyd. New York: Harper, 1984. Youngest-Younger

Lonesomeness is expressed through a prairie dog named Lester. Designed for easy reading or reading aloud.

LOUIE by Ezra Jack Keats. Illus. by the author. New York: Greenwillow, 1983. (Reissue of the 1975 publication) Youngest

A demonstration of a shy child substituting an inanimate object for live companionship. Louie's first friend is a puppet he made.

LUCIE BABBIDGE'S HOUSE by Sylvia Cassedy. New York: Thomas Y. Crowell, 1989. Middle-Older

Presented as a very withdrawn child, Lucy Babbidge is taunted by her classmates at Norwood Hall. They call her "goosey loosey" and report everything she does to the teacher. The teacher, Miss Pimm, portrayed as the most insensitive person one could find in such a position, is grossly stereotyped.

When Lucy goes "home" every afternoon from school, life is different. She retains a very special place in her family, where she feels loved and protected. There is Mumma, Dada, and younger brother Emmett. Also, the housekeeper and Mr. Broome are an extended part of the family.

A school assignment is used as the tool to add another dimension to Lucy's world. In response to the assignment by Miss Pimm, Lucy addresses her letter for a person of "renown" to Delia Hornsby, the designer of her "house." She doesn't expect an answer because Delia Hornsby is dead.

Skillfully, the author allows the reader to gradually realize that the house to which Lucy returns every afternoon is a doll house which she has discovered in the basement of the school. Her family are all imaginary. It is through her conversations with the dolls that the reader also recognizes that Lucy is not dumb, but possesses wit which may be beyond her years.

This book furnishes a gripping, unusual trip into the imaginary and magic. It presents a character whose tactics for survival seem almost schizophrenic. In the classroom and with the girls, Lucy is withdrawn, scared, and hopeless. With the dolls, she takes on voice and fantasizes about a loving family. The letters to Delia receive answers which can only be written by Lucy herself. Other stories place children in "outer" worlds where they find security, however, the reader is usually provided with some vehicle by which disbelief is suspended. Fantasy and realism, in this book, are fused in such a way that the character seems to take on two personalities.

In the end, Lucy's breakthrough is made evident when she responds to the teacher with a pun. She has formerly used such puns only as vocabulary for her imaginary brother. Adults may find this book disturbing, but it is possible that young readers will handle the "magic' and "fantasy' in their own way. There are many elements to be discussed. The stark picture of rejection and mistreatment of a "loner" should provoke response from most readers. Hope is offered when, finally, Lucy finds her "voice."

ME AND NESSIE by Eloise Greenfield. Illus. by Moneta Barnett, New York: HarperCollins, 1975 (reissued in paperback, 1984). Younger

This story, with psychological accuracy, presents a child who rids herself of an imaginary friend as she begins to attend school and make friends there.

MEDICINE WALK by Ardath Mayhar, New York: Atheneum, 1985. Middle-Older

In a small plane, Burr and his father are flying together over the petrified forest, when the father becomes ill. After bringing the plane in for a landing in the desert, the pilot-father dies. Burr realizes that he must leave the plane and his dead father to seek help. He takes meager supplies from on board the plane and sets out alone.

Facing the hazards of the desert, Burr recalls the teachings of an Apache foreman on his father's family ranch. The bits and pieces of information, remembered, help the boy to survive the excruciating trip through the desert to safety.

Some of the information recalled by Burr may seem a little far-fetched, but this remains a fairly good modern story of an individual using mental resources to survive a difficult circumstance. Such books give us a view of the combined forces of loneliness and aloneness diverted by the human instinct for survival.

MOVING MOLLY by Shirley Hughes. Illus. by the author. New York: Lothrop, Lee and Shepard, 1988. Younger

After moving, new friends help Molly deal with her loneliness. Details of the move are included. The busy family and Molly's eventual discovery of playmates are pictured in color.

MY FRIEND WILLIAM MOVED AWAY by Martha Whitmore
Hickman. Illus. by Bill Myers. New York: Abingdon, 1979.
Youngest

Moving or having a friend move away can sometimes bring to
the very young their first real feelings of loneliness. In this story,
Jimmy feels very much alone after William moves away.

NEXT DOOR NEIGHBORS by Sarah Ellis. New York: McElderry, 1990. Middle

In a story about the new child in town, Peggy, a clergyman's
daughter seeks acceptance by telling a lie about owning a horse.
When the lie is exposed, she is ostracized by the other girls.
Because of her isolation, Peggy forms a friendship with a lonely
immigrant boy named George. The two outcasts spend time with a
Chinese gardener who lives in the basement of the house next door
to Peggy. Together, all three, Peggy, George, and the gardener
discover their inner strengths and gain courage to overcome the
barriers facing them.

Loneliness, in this case leads to unlikely alliances, but the
alliances are supportive and provide sustenance for each individual's growth.

A PLACE BETWEEN, by Suzanne Newton. New York: Viking,
1986. Middle-Older

The author uses the term "wilderness wandering" to describe
that time period between being a child and an adult, and the time of
hesitancy between the old and the new. Absent from the small
North Carolina town where she grew up, Arden feels isolated and
alone. Ignored by her classmates in the new, big school, and facing
pressures from her grandmother regarding her tomboyish behavior, Arden yearns for the magic world of her younger years. Yet,
she knows that life has changed forever. Her grandfather has died,
and her father has lost his job. It is for these reasons that the family
has moved to grandmother's house.

At school, Arden meets Tyrone, a Black male fellow choir
member. Tyrone tries to make Arden feel more at home in her new
school, and with his help, Arden gradually begins the adjustment to
her new life.

When Arden returns home for a weekend visit with her old
friend, Dorjo, their friendship remains strong but the town and the

old house no longer feel like home. Shades of the old adage, "you can't go home again," are presented here. Lessons in replacing loneliness with new friends and activity are shown. This title is an independent sequel to "A Place Apart." The earlier title is more suspenseful and relationships seem more real. The association between Tyrone and Arden lacks the depth needed to promote caring. Being the only Black character, the designation of Tyrone as a choir singer is, to say the least, a slight bit stereotypical.

THE SECRET LIFE OF HUBIE HARTZEL by Susan Masters. Illus. by Gretchen Will Mayo. New York: Lippincott, 1990. Younger-Middle

Many readers will identify with Hubie who finds himself in a bad situation at home and at school. He is overweight, failing math, and is afraid of the class bully, Ralph Marruci. Hubie is the middle child, with a very spoiled younger sister and a pesky older sister. Hubie escapes by daydreaming which gets him into more trouble in his classes, but in the end, he finds a method to get even. This is a simple, straightforward, situational story for the young.

SONYA'S MOMMY WORKS by Arlene Alda. Illus. by the author. New York: Messner, 1983. Youngest

Presents images of the working mom while dealing with the feelings of aloneness a child experiences when mother first begins work. Illustrated with photographs.

TAWNY by Chas Carner. Illus. by Donald Carrick. New York: Macmillan, 1978. Middle-Older

This book deals with that special aloneness experienced by a child who loses a twin. After his brother's death, the boy in this story begins to find ways to fill lonely moments. One day he rescues an injured deer and cares for it. Later, he faces the challenge of returning the deer to the wild. The release of the deer, at the end, may be used by the author as a metaphor for the child releasing his brother.

THE TRIAL OF ANNA COTMAN by Vivien Alcock. New York: Delacorte, 1990. Middle-Older

Anna Cotman is presented as having a pleasant personality but feeling alone and friendless in her new setting. At first, she is pleased when Linda Miller, an unattractive classmate claims her for a friend. Later, Anna realizes that, in her fervor to belong, she has allowed Linda to involve her with some very unscrupulous characters.

Linda has encouraged Anna to join the "Society of Masks," a secret organization. Members wear costumes with masks and act out rituals. Soon, Anna notices and resents the way females in the club are treated by the boys. Observing other suspicious actions of club members, Anna confronts Linda and wishes to withdraw. Subsequently, the true and negative nature of the "club" is exposed. Young, lonely, and vulnerable boys are forced to steal to maintain membership.

Important here is the fact that loneliness can cause young people to accept unhealthy offers for companionship and belonging. The warnings are not blatant but through Anna's discoveries become definite as the story evolves. (Also PEER PRESSURES)

I. THE INDIVIDUAL

Feelings

All good novels include some definition of feelings through characterization. Sometimes these emotions are seen or felt through a character's actions. Anger, pathos, pity and other feelings can be aroused in the reader by an author's description of actions taken against a character. Authors provoke sympathy for characters in various ways—having them look different, having them fail in an endeavor, having them love someone from a distance, or having them experience a personal tragedy. In this section, the search was for those novels and stories which inadvertently provide insights to and understandings of human emotions—not only feelings which are casual to certain actions but also those which affect attitudes toward and responses to others. For young children, some books actually center on the definition and understanding of simple emotions like jealousy, fear, hate, and love, while appropriately older novels reveal understandings of these through the characters.

ARE YOU SAD, MAMA? by Elizabeth Winthrop. Illus. by Donna Diamond. New York: Harper and Row, 1979. Youngest

One of the few books for very young children designed to help them understand that adults have feelings too. In the story a young girl tries to make her mother feel better.

THE BEST WAY OUT by Karyn Follis Cheatham. New York: Harcourt Brace Jovanovich, 1982. Older

Characters are not deeply drawn in this story, but information combined with the situations presented, indicate feelings. Haywood is thirteen years old and on his second round of seventh grade. His prospects for going to high school and finishing are not

18

good. Being bused from the inner city to a middle class school, Haywood feels lost. There is a further downhill pull to his life when he crushes his finger in a bus accident.

As a final resort, counselors place Haywood in a special class led by a teacher named Ashley. At first, Haywood resents being in the class, but through the teacher's creative approach to learning, Haywood takes a new interest in his work. The individual attention received helps Haywood begin development toward his potential.

BOAT SONG by Frances Ward Weller. New York: Macmillan, 1987. Middle

Jonno and the bagpiper, Rob Lord, are the characters most emotionally revealed in this story. Jonno follows the sounds of the eerie music he hears on the beach. The strange sounds floating through the air capture his imagination and he follows the music until he discovers Rob Lord and his bagpipes. Jonno finds Rob to be a gruff yet understanding friend. Beyond his fascination with the bagpipes, Jonno's friendship with Rob is as strong as his current ambivalence toward his father. Jonno's alienation from his father does not lessen as Rob teaches him songs, and tells him stories from the highlands.

As in many stories about growing up, an older person is chosen by the author as the one who will relate to the young child seeking answers. The bagpiper has entered Jonno's life at a moment when he has become very frustrated about his father's expectations of him. Because his relationships with family and friends are edgy, Jonno transfers his affections to Rob until he realizes that Rob is also human. When the old man yells at him, Jonno thinks he has lost a friend.

On a foggy evening, Jonno accidently becomes lost offshore in a rowboat and is saved by following the sounds of the bagpipes on shore. Rob, realizing the danger of the situation, has purposefully played music to guide the boy to shore. With the help of Rob and the boating incident, the author allows Jonno opportunities to realize that friendship should not be banished by one angry encounter. He also realizes that his father cares for him.

THE BOSSING OF JOSIE by Ronda Armitage. Illus. by David Armitage. New York; Dutton, 1980. Youngest

Documenting that the youngest in the family also have feelings, this is the story of Josie who resents being bossed around by everyone in the family except the baby.

DADDY IS A MONSTER . . . SOMETIMES by John Steptoe. Illus.
by the author. New York: Harper and Row, 1980. Youngest

Two boys talk about their "monster" fathers but decide upon
evaluation that on balance their daddies may not be so mean.
Illustrated with the stylized drawings common to the author.

DARK AND FULL OF SECRETS by Carol Carrick. Illus. by
Donald Carrick. New York: Clarion Books, 1984. Younger

The "Christopher" stories about a boy and his dog will be
familiar to many young children. This one deals with fear of the
underwater and seems emotionally accurate. The watercolor illustrations add to the mood of the story. Lessons in diving and some
safety warnings are a natural part of the story.

DON'T HURT ME MAMA by Muriel Stanek. Illus. by Helen
Cogancherry. New York: Whitman, 1983. Younger-Middle

This story of child abuse designed for the very young might be
better used with older children and adults, although abuse is seen
through the eyes of a small child.

EVEN IF I DID SOMETHING AWFUL by Barbara Shook Hazen.
Illus. by Nancy Kincade. New York: Atheneum, 1981.
Youngest

Many young children will identify with the apprehensive girl
who is afraid of what will happen when she breaks her mother's
vase. Will mother still love her? In order to find answers, the child
asks her mother about other imaginary and problematic events. The
mother's answers are loving but also cite responsibility.

FITCHETTS FOLLY by Colby Rodowsky. New York: Farrar,
Straus and Giroux, 1987. Middle-Older

Emotions and feelings are constantly evident in this story set at
Taggart's Cove, sometime in the past. The characters play out
sentiments, described only through actions.
Sarah experiences and feels the agony of grief after the sudden
loss of her father. He drowns in an unsuccessful attempt to rescue
a family from a boat which has run aground. Only one member of
the family survives, Faith Wilkinson, who is about Sarah's age.

Sarah's feelings of grief are soon supplanted by those of jealousy when Faith comes to live at her home. Sarah sulks as Faith seems to capture the attention of everyone including Sarah's stepmother (Aunt Mom), her best friend, and her younger brother.

With these emotions smoldering, Sarah is sent to work in the local hotel where she meets rich Mrs. Conrad. At first, Sarah fantasizes about living with the Conrads, but later decides it would be better if they would take Faith away. She could then reclaim her place with family and friends. When her plans to rid herself of Faith fall apart and Sarah realizes that the Conrads are very shallow people, with disappointment and anger Sarah attacks Faith. Cruelly, she blames Faith for her father's death.

The story's resolution is sudden and somewhat melodramatic. In reaction to Sarah's accusation, Faith runs off to Fitchetts Folly, an unsafe part of the Cove, and Sarah feeling guilty tries to save her. Except for the slightly unsatisfying ending, the story is well told. Characters are not as "real" as they could have been, but the story itself is driven by the emotions felt by Sarah.

FLY FREE by C. S. Adler. New York: Coward-McCann, 1984. Middle-Older

This is primarily a story about a disfunctional family, but the main character's feelings of loneliness and low self-worth are poignantly portrayed. Thirteen-year-old Shari spends many hours alone fleeing the wrath of her emotionally disturbed mother. Her father, a trucker, is necessarily away for long periods. Shari loves her brother, but needs some personal support. This she finds when she establishes a friendship with an older woman, and when she is assured of her stepfather's love

FRED'S FIRST DAY by Cathy Warren. Illus. by Pat Cummings. New York: Lothrop, Lee and Shepard, 1984. Younger

For very young children the feelings of the middle sibling are explored. Fred is too old to play with his baby brother and too young to be a companion for his older brother. His problems are resolved when he goes to school. Illustrations are in full color.

I HATE MY BROTHER HARRY by Crescent Dragonwagon. Illus. by Dick Gackenbach. New York: HarperCollins, 1983. Youngest

Familiar fluctuating feelings between siblings are explored as a young girl states her negative feelings about her older brother. She does change her mind.

I'LL PROTECT YOU FROM THE JUNGLE BEASTS by Martha Alexander. New York: Dial, 1983. Youngest

Having a teddy bear as a companion helps a young boy conquer his fears while walking through the woods.

JACOB HAVE I LOVED by Katherine Paterson. New York: Crowell, 1980. Older-Oldest

Feelings are constantly evident in this novel about sibling rivalry. Louise is portrayed as the older (by minutes) twin sister of Caroline. Louise is darker, stronger and often forgotten as the attention in conversation and actions is paid to the fair-haired, talented Caroline. Living in the shadow of her sister is painful and fatefully several situations indicate to Louise that she is the lesser of the two.

The setting is in the 1940s on a tiny Chesapeake Bay Island. This area vulnerable to storms from the sea is the perfect background for the volatile feelings emerging in the story.

With all of the characters fleshed out to be real personalities, the feelings and conflicts of the main character become even more real. Louise faces the neglect of her parents, low feelings of self esteem, taunting and contempt from her elderly and senile grandmother, and adolescent sexual awakening when attracted to a much older man. She deals with these agonies while her insensitive sister excels at singing, is loved by everyone, and is given deference by the family and friends.

Finally, the author uses a confrontation with her mother as the catalyst for Louise to move away from her situation and to establish herself in the outer world of school, pursuing dreams of being a doctor. The reader learns that Louise does find her place in life—marries and has a child of her own while working as a nurse in the Appalachian mountains of West Virginia. Told from Louise's point of view, this is one of the few novels for young people which follows the young person through adolescence into adulthood. (This story also provides various images of women with Caroline retaining some memories and her nuturing instincts, but, emerging as the strongest.)

LAST ONE HOME, by Mary Pope Osborne. New York: Dial, 1986. Older

People assume that twelve year old Bailey Evans, who lives with her father and brother, is a tough kid. With a dry sense of humor and wisecracking manners, she manages to keep her feelings hidden. Bailey has been deliberate in her efforts to act grown-up, after her parents divorced and her mother moved away to Miami.

Recent events again disturb the status quo. Bailey's brother is leaving for the military and even worse her dad is serious about marrying saccharin, goody-goody Janet. Bailey feels alone while attempting to keep her world from falling apart. Her distress leads to meddling and causes her to alienate the people she loves. No matter where she turns at this point, she can't find what she wants—understanding, support, and consideration of her needs. Finally, the family has to rescue her from an attempt to run away. They find her at the bus station and try to make amends.

There is no happy ending—just Bailey's resignation to change. She determines to make the best of it and to begin planning for her own adult future.

Through a believable protaganist and the skillfully chosen cast surrounding her, the author ably provides insight into adolescent failings, resulting from traumatic changes and hiding one's thoughts and feelings. The interplay between characters shows realistic cause and effect.

MARIA THERESA by Mary Atkinson. Illustrated by Christine Engla Eber. Carrboro, NC.: Lollipop Power, 1979. Younger-Middle

A contemporary story of a young Chicana moving to a small midwestern town where she is faced with discrimination for the first time in her life. Her puppet Monteja helps her handle her emotions. It is the puppet which becomes the catalyst for Maria's gradual establishment of friendships.

The story is slight, and the premise is strained but some elements of culture are introduced including Maria's use of Spanish with the puppet.

MAUD FLIES SOLO by Gibbs Davis. Scarsdale, N.Y.: Bradbury Press, 1981. Middle

Feelings about growing apart from a sibling are humorously, yet poignantly, explored in this title. Maud is distressed by the increasing wedge between herself and her older sister. Her sister now has new friends and secrets that she will not share. Poor Maud doesn't understand why Lily is rejecting her. Maud's attempts to reconnect with her sister provide for some funny scenes.

One of the story's most humorous incidents happens when the older sister, Lily, and her friend join church and prepare for baptism. Being baptized is the "in" thing to do. Maud volunteers to be their helper, watching their clothing and towels. The resulting baptismal scenario when the clothes are lost is hilarious. But in spite of the humor, the issue of separation from a sibling because of age differences is clear. Many children will identify with this kind of emotional and real loss.

THE MOONLIGHT MAN by Paula Fox. New York: Bradbury Press. 1986. Older

The author reveals Catherine's outrage, humiliation, fear, and love as she spends time with her father who drinks too much.

Catherine's mother and father are divorced and she attends a boarding school for girls. Her father, a writer, travels continually and entices Catherine with adventurous offers, but has failed to fulfill his promises. Yet, Catherine expectantly awaits this summer's stay with her father, until he is hours late arriving to pick her up. When her father finally makes arrangements for Catherine to meet him, she finds him drunk.

In spite of this tenuous beginning, some moments of the trip are fun for Catherine. The father is a clinically proven example of the two faces of an alcoholic. Dad cooks for Catherine and takes her on a fishing trip. He promises not to drink but that promise is not kept. On one occasion, Catherine seeks help from the local minister when her father falls into a drunken stupor.

In the end, Catherine reluctantly calls her mother and asks to return home vowing never to tell about the traumatic experience with her father.

NIGHT CRY by Phyllis Reynolds Naylor. New York: Atheneum, 1984. Middle

Strong in its variety of characterizations, this is the story of a young girl suffering from the fear of her dead brother's horse. The setting and colorful characters add power to this suspenseful story. The protagonist overcomes her fears and superstitions to save a young boy who has been kidnapped.

THE NIGHT-LIGHT by Jane Feder. Illus. by Lady McCrady. New
   York: Dial, 1980. Youngest

Presents the familiar theme of a child's fear of the dark in
acceptable form for the youngest.

NUISANCE by Fredericka Berger. New York: William Morrow,
   1983. Middle.

Feelings are adequately dealt with in this book about a child
facing the traumas resulting from her parent's divorce and her
mother's remarriage. Julie, the main character, gains some sense of
balance when she makes new friends at a new school.

ONE-EYED CAT by Paula Fox. Scarsdale, N.Y.: Bradbury Press,
   1984. Middle-Older

This mysterious and disturbing story deals with a young boy's
feelings of guilt, when he disobeys his father and shoots the gift
rifle, sent by his uncle. The child is haunted by the secret he must
keep, knowing that when he shot, he hit something, the one-eyed
cat. Unlike many books for children, the adult characters have
depth, making the boy's dilemma even more real. His mother is a
partial invalid and his father is a minister. The old man next door
helps him care for the cat. Each adult presents him with the
questions about right and wrong. Through them and his own
introspection, the boy finds answers.

SOMETHING TO COUNT ON by Emily Moore. New York:
   Dutton, 1980. Middle

An understanding teacher and a strong, gentle mother are
catalysts for ten-year-old Lorraine's emotional growth. When her
mother and father are divorced, she vents her feelings of anger on
almost everyone. She constantly gets into trouble at school and at
home is equally sullen and argumentative. The adjustment is
gradual and seems real.

SPIDERS IN THE FRUIT CELLAR by Barbara M. Joosse. Illus. by
   Kay Chorao. New York: Alfred A. Knopf, 1983. Youngest

When sent to the cellar for a jar of fruit, Elizabeth has to
overcome her fear of spiders. Mother takes a very tactful approach

to the child's fears. She tells Elizabeth how spiders are helpful and allows the child to help in other ways until she can conquer her fears.

TAKING TERRI MUELLER by Norma Fox Mazer. New York: Avon Flare, 1981. (New York: Morrow, 1983, hardcover) Older

For as long as she can remember, thirteen-year-old Terri and her father have moved from place to place. They have travelled all over the country, never settling anywhere longer than a few months. Until now, Terri has believed that her mother was killed in a car accident, but soon, she is led to believe that her father has lied to her. Eventually Terri learns that her mother is indeed alive and that her father kidnapped her after their divorce.

Terri's reunion with her mother is difficult, as is the reconciliation of her feelings for her father. Terri's characterization is believable but the adults are drawn with too little depth for a serious understanding of issues relating to child stealing. The book could provide the vehicle for more healthy discussion of the issues.

THAT'S NOT FAIR! by Gyo Fujikawa. Illus. by the author. New York: Grosset and Dunlap, 1983. Youngest

For schoolrooms and homes this is a handy book about friends who quarrel and then make up. This author has produced several other titles focusing on socialization.

TURKEYLEGS THOMPSON, by Jean McCord. New York: Atheneum, 1979. Middle-Older

After her father left, Betty Ann Thompson assumed care of the younger children, so that her mother could work and support the family. Now she goes to school, takes care of her baby sister, and supervises her younger brother. Betty often brawls with those who have dubbed her "Turkeylegs," and who tease when her brother wets his pants.

Life becomes even more complicated when "Turkeylegs" steals a bike and takes her sister for a ride. In a fall, she accidently hurts her sister's leg. The injury doesn't seem serious, but later on when her sister dies, Betty Ann blames herself. She feels resentment when her wayward father comes home for the funeral. She is also miffed by the improvement in her brother's behavior, with the father present.

Mourning her sister's death and feeling hostile toward her father, Betty Ann runs away to a secret hiding place in the hills. She shares her distress with a boy whom she has met there earlier. Her friend gives advice which helps her to return home with a new perspective on life.

Many emotions are explored here including feelings of rejection, anger, and sorrow.

THE VERY BEST OF FRIENDS by Margaret Wild. Illus by Julie
    Vivas. New York: Harcourt Brace Jovanovich (Gulliver
    Books), 1990. Middle

Although presented simply, this story of relationships, love, and loss may be disturbing to some. James and Jessie are a farm couple with no children. James spends his days together with his beloved cat, William.

When James dies, Jessie rejects the cat, and retreats into her own lonely sorrow. The cat struggles for attention and finally gets it by scratching Jessie.

Since very young children (for whom this book is designed) will identify with the cat, the thoroughly portrayed rejection may be too much for them to handle, but the process of rejecting others while grieving is real and this book could be used with older children and parents.

THE VILLAGE BY THE SEA by Paula Fox. New York: Franklin
    Watts (Orchard Books), 1988. Middle-Older

Adult characters and issues are more apparent in this book than in many for young children, although the main character is a young girl. Ten-year-old Emma discovers much about Aunt Bea and Uncle Crispin when she is sent to live with them. Emma travels to the huge log house by the sea to live with her aunt and uncle while her father has heart surgery. Uncle Crispin makes her welcome but Emma doesn't understand her aunt's fluctuating moods and attitudes. She also doesn't understand the complex relationship between her uncle and aunt, at one moment loving and at another stormy.

Emma's disconsolate feelings are relieved by the friendship she forms with Bertie, a young girl who lives nearby. They spend long hours building their own village by the sea from bits of shell, rocks, sand, etc.

Gradually, it is disclosed that Aunt Bea is an alcoholic, when Emma finds several small plastic deer which are discarded bottle tops. Emma still has no realization of the depth of the problem. What she knows is how her aunt makes her feel. The worst anger and disappointment is felt when her aunt destroys the village Emma and Bertie have built. Innocently, the girls have used one of the plastic deer as scenery for their beachside village.

Returning home after her father has healed, Emma's feelings about her Aunt and Uncle are uncertain. She finds this addition to her diary written by her aunt. "Aunt Bea is a sad, bad old woman."

Some of the nuances of the relationship between the adults will not be understood by children, but they will clearly relate to Emma's feelings.

WAITING by Nicki Weiss. Illus. by the author. New York: Greenwillow, 1984. Youngest.

Annalee waits alone for her mother to return. The mixed feelings and emotions of waiting and anticipation are shown through the illustrations. Many young children will identify with Annalee's feelings and will be happy when mother does return.

WHAT DO YOU DO WHEN YOUR MOUTH WON'T OPEN? by Susan Beth Pfeffer. Illus. by Lorna Tomei. New York: Yearling Books, 1981. Younger

Children and adults will identify with the fear of speaking in front of a group. Although dealt with humorously, this book reasonably covers the subject.

WORDS BY HEART by Quida Sebestyen. New York: Little, Brown and Co., 1979. Older

Lena, a young Black girl, is determined to win the spelling bee and to excel in the narrow-minded, bigoted community in which she lives. Facing ignorance and racism, the family members are stalwart in their efforts to do well. Their success leads to violence and the death of Lena's beloved father.

Lena's courage is the strongest aspect of this award-winning and controversial novel. Her father's inability to feel anger at the mistreatment of his daughter and himself is unbelievable. The extremes of action and emotion wrought by racism are evident, but the Black family is placed in a situation where there is no resource available to them but themselves. This is clearly one example of an author's ability to evoke feelings in the reader through actions, but the necessary understandings of human feelings are not provided through the characters. (For discussions and examinations of this title see: "Words by Heart, a Black Perspective" by Rudine Sims, in Interracial Books for Children, vol 11 (1980), no. 7, pp. 12–17, and other commentaries in the same issue.)

THE YEAR THE SUMMER DIED by Patricia Lee Gauch. New York: Putnam, 1985. Older

For fourteen-year-old Erin, summer visits with her grandparents have always been pleasant. She looks forward this year to seeing her friend Laurie, with whom she has had many summers of fun. In years past, one of her joys was playing an imaginary game of cowgirls with Laurie.

Upon arrival at her grandparent's home, Erin finds everything changed. Laurie has grown up, and is in love with a local boy. Only tolerating Erin, Laurie finds no time to play the old childish games. Also, Erin is faced with her grandfather's disgruntled attitude, aggravated by someone entering and stealing from his boat house.

Erin experiences those feelings of loneliness caused when friends are torn apart. This separation of friends, brought on by their age difference, may be symbolized by the tornado which tears the town apart. For Erin, summer will never be the same, but her love for her grandparents and her summer retreat remain.

1. THE INDIVIDUAL

Individual Growth and Development
(Images of Self and Others)

Robert Coles in his book CHILDREN OF CRISIS, published in the sixties, examined children's perceptions of themselves and others through the children's drawings. He found disturbing evidence that children internalize society's negative and positive images of race. He wrote, "I am also saying that the way these children draw is affected by their racial background, and what that fact means in their particular world (society) at that particular time (period of history)." Books may represent only a minor influence in such image building, but they can help establish and amplify both negative and positive images children may have of themselves and others. Before such views are strongly embedded, negative images may be questioned through an author's strong and positive counter portrayals. In the selected titles below, images of various racial groups, of the aged, and of other cultures are seen as presented in works of fiction. Also included are titles in which children themselves improve in self perspective and/or self esteem.

AMISH ADVENTURE by Barbara Smucker. Scottdale, PA: Herald Press, 1983. Younger

The story, itself, is not as good as the view of life in an Amish family, and the images of a different way of life portrayed positively.

ANGEL SQUARE by Brian Doyle. New York: Bradbury Press, 1984. Younger

This story for young readers takes and unusual approach to the subject of racial intolerance. Set in French Canada, readers are introduced to a community of French Canadians, Irish Catholics, and Jews. The problems which ensue stem from nonacceptance of cultural differences. This message is couched in the humorous and successful sleuthing of a child who follows the radio mystery show, THE SHADOW. Tommy, the sleuth, undertakes solving the mystery of who brutalized Sammy Rosenburg's father. A man in a hood attacked Mr. Rosenburg because he was Jewish. Tommy solves the mystery and exposes the culprit.

CHILD OF THE MORNING by Barbara Corcoran. New York: Atheneum, 1982. Middle-Older

A fictionally capsuled view of a handicap, not often dealt with, is offered. Susan suffers from epilepsy as a result of a head injury. The problem is dealt with realistically and no pat solutions are presented, but readers gain a better understanding of an illness around which many myths are built.

FINDING DAVID DOLORES by Margaret Willey. New York: Harper and Row, 1986. Older-Oldest

In her thirteenth year, Arly becomes a different person, rejecting her mother, becoming a loner, developing a low self image, and allowing her grades to deteriorate. Life has lost its meaning until Arly catches a glimpse of David Dolores, and from a distance she falls head over heels in love. As her obsession develops, Arly tracks David, observing him whenever she can, and falling more madly in love. After discovering that David plays the oboe, Arly encourages her father to buy one for her, hoping eventually this will help her make an impression on David. Her fantasies are all her own until Regina arrives at school.

The author establishes that the new girl, Regina, is different when she shows up at school in a silk dress while all the other pupils are wearing jeans. Arly is intrigued with Regina and maneuvers a relationship with her. The friendship between two loners seems perfect to Arly until it becomes evident that some very disturbing things are going on in Regina's life. Arly is startled when Regina denies her parentage. The friendship becomes combative when Regina maneuvers an entrance to David's home and forms an unhealthy attachment to David's mother.

Still quietly worshipping David, Arly resents Regina's lies and manipulation, but she doesn't know how to extricate herself from the situation. David resents the attachment Regina has formed to his mother and, eventually, this brings about communication between him and Arly. By the time the final traumatic scenes develop, the two of them are at least friendly. Through assessments of the entire situation, Arly learns and grows. She finds resources within herself which allow her to face Regina and to be a catalyst for the final resolution. When David goes away to music school, Arly has come out of her shell, has begun to communicate with her family again, and has gained in self esteem.

The author has provided a complex but sustained plot centered first on young love, but allowing the main character to grow in understanding of life from several angles.

GAFFER SAMSON'S LUCK by Jill Paton Walsh. Illus. by Brock Cole. New York: Farrar, Straus and Giroux, 1984. Middle

Excellent descriptions of the Fens and the characterization of Gaffer Samson are background for the story of a young boy surviving in a new setting.

James soon learns that there are strong class and economic divisions in the English village which is his new home. His first introduction to local ways is through Angey, who isn't allowed in the local store because she lives in the trailer (Gypsy) camp. Angey becomes his stalwart supporter as James faces the threats and bullying of the locals. The young boy is willing to risk the results of local ire in order to recover a lost "luck piece" for Gaffer Samson. He knows that the old man who lives next door and who has befriended him is dying. His hope is that the luck piece will bring healing to Gaffer. In James' effort to find Gaffer's "Luck" he gains the respect of his peers.

Although this story's focus is on the relationship between the young boy and the older man, there is a lot to be learned about the viciousness of societal stratas and social divisions.

GET ON OUT OF HERE, PHILIP HALL by Bette Greene. New York: Dial Press, 1981. Middle-Older

This sequel to PHILIP HALL LIKES ME, I RECKON, MAYBE, offers further insights to the process of growing up, through the escapades of Beth Lambert. These books do not present aspects of Black culture which emphasize differences. Instead, "shades" of culture are lightly portrayed through the nuances of actions and language. Therefore, readers can easily identify with Beth's feelings.

THE GIFT by Joan Lowery Nixon. Illus. by Andrew Glass. New York: Macmillan, 1983. Middle

In this realistic book about the relationship between a boy and his Irish great grandfather, the reader is introduced to Irish folklore. The search for a leprechaun moves the story from realism into a magical fantasy.

HANNAH'S ALASKA by Joanne Reiser. Illus. by Julie Downing. Milwaukee, Wisconsin: Carnival Press Books, 1983. Younger

This picture book with full color illustrations portrays simple episodes in the life of an Alaskan family.

HAZEL RYE by Vera and Bill Cleaver. New York: Lippincott, 1983. Middle-Older

The main character, Hazel Rye, is defined early as an independent, "know-it-all." She lives with her father on his Florida citrus farm. The two have established a special relationship into which the Poole family intrudes.

When the Pooles arrive needing a place to stay, Hazel rents them a small house on a portion of the groves which is a bequest from her father. She begins to relate to young Felder Poole, and the two of them work to save the dying trees in this portion of the farm.

Gradually Hazel faces several conflicts: the conflict with her father who resents the family's intrusion on their closeness; conflict within herself when she confronts her ignorance in contrast to the Pooles who are intellectually curious; and the conflict of her awakening need for associations beyond that with her father. Overall, this story presents a child who has to confront her own false sense of self.

HOTEL BOY by Curt and Gita Kaufman. Photos by Curt Kaufman. New York: Atheneum, 1987. Younger

Presents images from which many children can learn and with which some will identify. Black and white photos help to emphasize the starkness of life for a young boy and his family living in a welfare hotel.

HOW DOES IT FEEL TO BE OLD? by Norma Farber. Illus. by Trina S. Hyman. New York: Dutton, 1985. Youngest

A grandmother tries to help her granddaughter understand what it is like to be old.

I BE SOMEBODY by Hadley Irwin. New York: Atheneum, 1984. Middle-Older

Ten-year-old Rap, finds his everyday life in Clearview colored with mystery words such as ATHABASCA, mentioned in conversations between adults. These include his aunt, with whom he lives; the Creek Indian, who is like a grandfather to him; and others. The story evolves with Rap discovering more about the mystery words, about his father, and about his Aunt's wish to travel to ATHABASCA. The town of Athabasca, located in far away Alberta, Canada, has been settled by Blacks seeking a better life. In the year of 1910, Rap and his Aunt travel by train to the Canadian town.

Based on a little known fact of history, this is a worthwhile story of a boy's search for identity. The story, however, lacks some of the tension needed to involve the reader in Rap's search for the truth. There are fuzzy areas in the progressions and transitions of the plot. Even so, the story is good enough to use as a catalyst for discussion of this period in Black history. The images of Rap and family are mostly positive.

I KNOW A LADY by Charlotte Zolotow. Illus. by James Stevenson. New York: Greenwillow, 1984. Younger

Positive images of the aged are presented through Sally's relationship with and love for an old lady in her neighborhood.

JAMAICA'S FIND by Juanita Havill. Illus by Anne Sibley O'Brien. Boston: Houghton Mifflin, 1986. Younger

A young Black girl makes a "find" in the park which eventually brings her a new friend. The object found is a stuffed dog, eventually returned to its rightful owner. Simple views of a Black child and her family are juxtaposed with those of her white counterpart.

A JAR OF DREAMS by Yoshiko Uchida. New York: Atheneum, 1981. Older

Rinko Tsujimura is a twelve-year-old Japanese-American girl growing up in Berkeley, California during the depression. Sometimes she hates being Japanese and having a Japanese name, that no one will try to pronounce. Rinko feels like a "nothing" at school, where she is the only non-white. Uchida is subtle and brilliant in her presentation of Rinko's thoughts. The loneliness and underdeveloped sense of self-worth felt by this young child of immigrants are revealed painfully and accurately.

Along with the views of racism and isolation, different levels of association with whites are shown. The rich families in the Berkeley Hills love the "hardworking Japanese," while a neighbor sincerely befriends the family.

Rinko's family are faced with the financial hardships of the times complicated by a vicious attack mounted against them by the owner of a competing laundry. It is Rinko's aunt, visiting from Japan, who provides the family with the strength to go on in the face of these pressures. Using resources rooted in Japanese tradition, she helps them to move beyond their sense of powerlessness, to regain their confidence, and to renew their dreams. Rinko along with the rest of the family gains strength and through her the reader has a sense of hope.

Uchida's writing is beautifully descriptive, helping the reader to see and feel the characters, time and place. (Other titles by Uchida documenting Rinko's life are available.)

JUST US WOMEN by Jeanette Caines. Illus. by Pat Cummings. New York: Harper and Row, 1982. Younger

A young girl and her favorite aunt take a trip to North Carolina. Presented is a loving view of that special affection which can exist between a child and a special member of the family. The "two women" are shown having a picnic and shopping at a rummage sale. The pleasant somewhat romanticized illustrations add warmth to the text. Characters are Black.

KIM KIMI by Hadley Irwin. New York: McElderry, 1987. Older

Kim Yogushi's Japanese father is dead. She is now Kim Andrews and torn because she looks Japanese but knows little about her culture and her father's family. Without permission, she makes a trip to San Francisco to seek her roots and her father's people. Kim learns that the family objected when her father married his Caucasian college sweetheart. From members of the family she also begins to learn, gradually, what it means to be Japanese in America.

The story is sometimes awkward and unrealistic. The character of Mrs. Muller, the Dungeon Master, is probably introduced to keep Kim from being a true runaway. Kim's brother tells Mrs. Muller about Kim's plans to visit San Francisco. Being taken to the site of an internment camp on her first visit with her father's family also seems unreal. There is such a need for books which deal with the issues facing children of mixed parentage, but this title fails in many ways. Some cultural information can be gained through Kim's San Francisco visit.

THE NIGHT JOURNEY by Kathryn Lasky. Illus. by Trina Schart Hyman. New York: Frederick Warne, 1981. Middle-Older

A young Jewish girl finds out about her past from her ailing grandmother. The grandmother's story of escape from persecution in Russia is juxtaposed with views of Rachel's current life and family. The grandmother's tale of survival and escape from Czarist Russia, "the night journey," will hold readers spellbound.

NOW ONE FOOT, NOW THE OTHER by Tomie de Paola. Illus. by the author. New York; Putnam, 1981. Youngest

An unusual but realistic view of the aged as Bobby helps his grandfather who is recovering from a stroke. Grandfather has told stories about his helping Bobby learn to walk. Now the roles are reversed.

PIE-BITER by Ruthanne Lum McCunn. Illus. by You-shan Tang. Design Enterprises of San Francisco, 1983. Younger

Through the legend of PIE-BITER young readers are introduced to the historical period of the 1860s in the United States. While working to build railroads, Pie-Biter ate pies instead of rice to gain strength.

R-T, MARGARET, AND THE RATS OF NIMH by Jane L. Conly. Illus. by Leonard Rubin. New York: HarperCollins Children's Books, 1990. Middle-Older

This title may seem a strange one for inclusion in this section. It is included because of the considerable growth which is allowed in the main character.

Overweight and sullen, Margaret resents the way her family's life has to revolve around her younger brother Artie, who can't speak because of an illness he had as a baby. On a camping trip the two children get lost and are discovered by Christopher (from *Rasco and the Rats of NIMH*, 1986).

The fantasy-adventure allows Margaret to grow as an individual. She gains self esteem through her ability to assist the rats. She also observes how the rats relate to Artie. When they return home Margaret is a better person because of her experience.

THE RUNNER by Cynthia Voigt. Illus. by Leonard Rubin. New
   York: Atheneum, 1985. Older-Oldest

Bullet Timmerman defines himself by running. When he is angry at the way people try to "box him in," he runs. When his mother belittles him and refuses to stand up for him, he runs. He serves on the school cross country team but only on his own terms. Not being a team player, he is isolated from his teammates. Approaching everyone with a wall of scorn, he has no friends except his employer, Patrice.

When the running coach asks him to assist a Black runner, Bullet quits the team. It is Patrice who helps Bullet to face and overcome his prejudices and to unlock some of the pain which has led to his attitude toward life and people.

SAMURAI OF GOLD HILL by Yoshiko Uchida. Illus. by Ati
   Forberg. Creative Arts Book Co., 1985. Middle-Older

This is a fictionalized account of the founding of the first Japanese settlement in California. The story chronicles the decision to leave Japan and the terrible struggles the settlers faced upon arrival. Told from the perspective of a fourteen-year-old boy, the narrative explains that Koichi has been a member of the last powerful family to fall to the emperor in 1868. Koichi is a samurai boy, born into nobility. He has been trained to function in a world of privilege but that life has crumbled as he faces his new life in California. The author speaks through Koichi's inner feelings of his struggles, and of his recognition that his former way of life will never return.

SONORA BEAUTIFUL by Lucille Clifton. Illus. by Michael
   Garland. New York: Dutton, 1981. Middle

The false standards of beauty in our society are unreachable for most young girls and even more remote for Blacks. This story presents the meaning of beauty to a child who thinks she is ugly. The subject is nicely dealt with. Hopefully similar efforts will be made at an older level.

TODAY'S SPECIAL: Z.A.P. AND ZOE by Athena V. Lord. Illus. by Jean Jenkins. New York: Macmillan, 1984. Middle

Offered here is a view of a Greek immigrant family in a small town (Cohoes) in New York State during 1939. Most children will be interested in the everyday experiences while learning a bit about Greek culture. Humor abounds in the story and illustrations.

TOUGH BEANS by Betty Bates. Drawings by Leslie Morrill. New York: Holiday House, 1988. Younger

When Nat Berger learns that he has diabetes, he takes charge of his life and the routines he must perform. But he doesn't allow his confrontation with the disease to keep him from facing life as a normal boy—and even fighting his neighbor and bully Jasper Denletter.

VISITING MISS PIERCE by Pat Derby. New York: Farrar, Straus and Giroux, 1986. Middle-Older

Images of the elderly are offered in many titles, but few show those in convalescent homes. In this story, a teenager becomes involved with a senile woman in a convalescent home, as the result of a school project. She tells him stories about her brother Willie. The resulting relationship is touching and sometimes humorous.

WHEN I WAS YOUNG IN THE MOUNTAINS by Cynthia Rylant. Illus. by Diane Goode. New York: Dutton, 1982. Youngest

Younger readers are offered a view of love amid poverty in this story of a grandmother and two children, set in Appalachia. Images of various elements of hill culture are apparent through the foods, a baptism, the country store, and quiet times on the front porch. A gentle, positive story.

1. THE INDIVIDUAL

Sexuality

In an essay about children's books titled, "Of Good Courage," Anne Devereaux Jordan suggests that, "Questions such as 'Should I have a sexual relationship?' can conjure up as much fear for the adolescent as nightmares did for the preschooler, and attempting to find answers to such questions requires just as much courage as facing the imaginary monster." Facing the imaginary monster of sexuality in fiction for children and young adults still seems problematic for most authors and publishers. While statistics show that children are entering puberty at a younger age, many authors are not comfortable with presenting emotional and physical aspects of sexuality in their youthful characterizations. The increase of teenage pregnancies does not seem to be proportionately represented in teen novels. AIDS as a social and personal problem has appeared in several novels, but venereal diseases remain hidden. Presented in this section are selected titles, most of which are designed for older readers. Some are honest and deal realistically with the questioning process, while others seem self-conscious in their efforts to deal with this very natural aspect of young life.

ABBY MY LOVE by Hadley Irwin. New York: Atheneum, 1985.
    Older-Oldest

This story introduces the problem of incest, but avoids some of the central feelings by having the story told by the victim's boyfriend. From this point of view, the story is well told and the suggestion at the end that incest becomes a family problem is realistic.

Chip is in love with Abby and he believes that she likes him. He can't understand her changes from acceptance to rejection of him. The story moves gradually to Chip's discovery that Abby is being sexually abused by her father. Her mysterious actions earlier in the story are thus explained.

The resolution is somewhat realistic, when Chip tells his parents the secret and Abby's parents confront the problem by going to counseling. The real pain that Abby must have experienced is never revealed.

ANNIE ON MY MIND by Nancy Garden. New York: Farrar, Straus and Giroux, 1982. Older-Oldest

The story of Liza, a very bright high school senior, and Annie, equally bright but less privileged. The two form a close friendship which turns into love.

Liza narrates the story telling how she feels about Annie. She discusses her confusion and her inability to believe she could have sexual feelings for a woman. Liza's words are very believable. The language the author provides realistically portrays a young eighteen-year-old woman concerned with her sexual feelings. She is afraid of what her parents and friends will think of her when she confesses that she is gay, while simultaneously questioning her own future.

CRAZY VANILLA by Barbara Werbsa. New York: Harper and Row, 1986. Older-Oldest

Tyler Woodruff is from a privileged family which lives in Hampton at the end of Long Island, New York. He and his brother Cameron have always been close until he learns that Cameron is gay.

A tidal wave of emotion breaks loose in the Woodruff family when elder Mr. Woodruff accidently opens a letter to Cameron from David exposing Cameron's homosexuality. Tyler tries to handle the news graciously, while his father goes on a rampage.

When Cameron is banished from the house, Tyler is left alone to deal with his feelings of confusion and love. Over the years, Tyler has been very much a loner spending most of his time photographing birds. He continues his photography jaunts while trying to sort out his feelings about Cameron. During one of his ventures he meets Mitzi, who is tough, poor and also loves photography. Through the growing relationship with Mitzi, Tyler begins to confront his feelings about Cameron.

The friendship between Mitzi and Tyler is a study in contrasts, rich versus poor and worldly versus sheltered. Even their photographs are opposites, Tyler's are romantic and Mitzi's are bleak.

While Tyler learns a lot about life from Mitzi, she only allows her tough veneer to crack slightly. This is probably appropriate because eventually, Mitzi moves on with her mother and the latest of her mother's boyfriends. All is not well with Tyler, but he at least feels ready to reestablish communication with his brother.

The issue of sexuality is not central to this story but it is an important element. The family's reaction to Cameron's secret seems realistic.

FIRST THE EGG by Louise Moeri. New York: Dutton, 1982. Older-Oldest

This fictitious story is based on the findings of a real experiment held in high schools around the country. The students in a parenting class are given an egg which they are to perceive as a new baby. They are paired and told to keep a diary of the (baby's) egg's progress, and are also informed that the egg should never be left alone.

Through the eyes of Sarah Webster, we view her own reaction and that of her partner, David Hanna. While dealing with the emotions raised by the egg assignment, Sarah simultaneously faces a storm of emotions exploding in her family. For the first time, she observes her parents as people, not fixtures. She also begins to recognize her own lack of interest in her younger sister's feelings.

Some of the real life actions which develop along with the egg assignment don't ring true. For example, David suddenly decides to travel to Mexico with friends and gets involved in selling drugs. Nothing about his characterization prepares the reader for this move and the story could have been complete without the incident. The episodes in Sarah's life are more believable. Discussions of the book and the experiment could lead to learning about the responsibilities of parenthood.

THE GIRL WHO WANTED A BOY by Paul Zindel. New York: Harper and Row, 1981. Older-Oldest

This is not the usual suburban romance story, nor are the characters drawn in a familiar way. Mother has many boyfriends and father is "alive and well working in Manhattan—and living with Pauline." Sister Maureen who has always been popular, is blond and bouncy and laments that her younger sister has not experienced sex.

These characters are the backdrop for Sibella's story of growing up. Sibella, herself, is different—she is a scientific whiz, has a gift for fixing things, and has two bank accounts earned from her "fix-it" jobs. But, what Sibella wants most in life is a boy. She dreams of having a loving relationship and records her fantasies in her diary.

After falling in love with his picture, she throws herself at Dan, who turns out to be a ne'r-do-well and drunk. She sees his picture in a newspaper ad for midget auto racing and is able to trace Dan's whereabouts. A rather one-sided and tenuous relationship develops.

Some of the characterizations are strong but the story falls flat. Sibella's obsession with Dan played out to the extreme of buying him a van seems unrealistic. The sexual encounter between the two happens after Dan has told her "If that's what you'd like, I wouldn't mind doing it. I've done it with a lot worse than you . . . you're not my dream come true. . . ." In spite of this, she thinks that the experience is wonderful, "as his lips touched hers she knew why she had been born," and discovers "what she was made for." Some of the expressions in Sibella's diary are poignant and could represent those of a teenager struggling with self image, however, a mother and sister so eager to have Sibella find a male would certainly have informed her about birth control. It is her father, instead, who says, "the only rules I would say you should follow are two: 'One, don't hurt anybody; and two, don't get knocked up.' "

When Dan leaves and Sibella faces what she has done, the story is near its end. She has decided to get over the shame and pain of having thrown herself at Dan and to seek for the kind of love that will last a lifetime. "And I'm only fifteen," she says.

HEY, KID! DOES SHE LOVE ME? by Harry Mazer. Crowell, 1984. Older-Oldest

This humorous story could be used to introduce the subjects of teenage pregnancy, loving, and parenting. Jeff, who dreams of being a movie director, is madly in love with Mary and Mary's baby Hannah. Told from Jeff's point of view, the story follows the developing relationship between the young eighteen year old and the unmarried teenage mother.

Jeff builds fantasies about Mary and himself becoming lovers, while becoming more and more attached to the baby. The relationship between Jeff and the baby is really the strength of the story. The hilarious scenes provided when Hannah is left in Jeff's care could be enlightening to males who have never accepted this kind of responsibility.

Through the relationship, the disappointment and final rejection by Mary, Jeff grows up a little. In the end, when he moves to the West Coast to pursue his dreams, and Mary is on the East Coast with a small acting troupe, the two write letters and remain friends.

A LITTLE LOVE by Virginia Hamilton. New York: Philomel Books, 1984. Older-Oldest

Sheena Hadley is overweight, terribly unhappy, and sometimes feels empty inside, while finding the father she has never known, is becoming an obsession. In moments of depression, food and a supportive, loving boyfriend are her solace.

As usual, Virginia Hamilton offers young people powerful characterizations, real situations, and confrontation with real emotions including sexual attraction. The portrayals of the elderly grandparents, who raised Sheila, and the family's confrontation with the some of the problems which accompany the aging process are sometimes funny and sometimes painful. While Sheena's agony concerning her father is consuming, her portrayal is not one dimensional. She loves her grandparents but hates having to be responsible for them as they age. She loves Forrest, but forces him to understand that she is not complete without knowledge of her father. She eats too much because of her emotional turmoil but is a good student at the vocational school which she attends.

When summer vacation comes, Sheena, with her boyfriend, Forrest, sets out to find her father in Forrest's old beat-up car. Sheena does find strength and love, but from Forrest instead of the wayward father. When the two make love, it is clear that they are making a commitment to share in unfettered physical and spiritual support.

MOTOWN AND DIDI, A Love Story by Walter Dean Myers. New York: Viking Kestrel, 1984. Older-Oldest

A powerful love story presents two teens growing up in Harlem. Walter Dean Myers provides the reader with the background of life in Harlem including deserted buildings in which Motown lives when he loses his job, the corner newsstand and its proprietor who has a special view of life in the neighborhood, and the bookstore and its owner who has a special affection for Motown.

When Didi enters the picture, the surrounding, violent, drug scene is introduced through Didi's brother Tony, who is gradually becoming hooked on drugs. Didi, a good student, represents the frustration of those who are struggling to rise above and move out of the squalor. But, Didi finds her efforts foiled when she doesn't receive a complete scholarship to college. When the scholarship does materialize, her mother is too sick to be left alone.

Within this setting and these conditions, an unlikely but believable loving relationship develops between Motown and Didi. Motown, who has been raised in foster homes and who struggles to make a way for himself, emerges as something of a hero. Didi searches for what is real when her escape valve of out-of-town schooling does not materialize. The author presents the relationship between the two as one which grows with gentle power amid turmoil and violence.

NIGHT KITES by M.E. Kerr. New York: Harper and Row, 1986
    Oldest

Erick's life is being torn apart by the secrets he must keep. His brother has AIDS and Erick is obsessed with his best friend's new girlfriend.

In the beginning Erick tries to control his growing passion for Nicki. Erick and Jack, both seventeen, have been best friends for years. Erick has his own girlfriend, Dill, who is the typical, wholesome, "pom pom" girl—no comparison to the sexy, well built, and different, Nicki.

Simultaneously the story of Erick's brother begins to develop. Pete has been suffering from diarrhea since he returned from a trip abroad. When he gets even sicker, he visits the doctor and finds out he has AIDS. As the family crisis develops, Erick's father exposes his rigidity and prejudices, blaming Erick's mom for Pete's homosexuality. He does not wish to desert his son, but he wants the facts about Pete's illness kept secret.

Meantime, Erick succumbs to Nicki's wiles and becomes sexually involved with her. Sworn to secrecy by his father, Erick has to keep his agonies about his brother hidden from her and from his best friend. He can't tell Jack or Dill about his relationship with Nicki.

Soon Erick finds himself friendless. Jack is angry upon discovery that Erick is sleeping with Nicki. Dill, of course, feels rejected and cheated.

This book is commendable in its attempt to deal with a family facing the illness and probable death of a child with AIDS. The anger and recriminations of the father are all too real, while Erick's quiet acceptance seems a little unreal. The most confusing part of the story is the juxtaposition of Erick's brother dying with AIDS against Erick's falling into bed with Nicki with no hint of his using any kind of protection. Obviously, the emphasis here is on the homosexual side of the AIDS problem. With AIDS spreading more and more into the heterosexual community, it seems irresponsible of the author not to have Erick face some of these questions about his sexual relationship with Nicki, especially since she is portrayed as a person who has had other sexual encounters. These are issues which can of course be discussed after reading the book.

THE PEOPLE THEREIN by Mildred Lee. New York: Houghton Mifflin, (Clarion Books), 1980. Older-Oldest

This novel does not deal directly with issues of sexuality, but it is a story about the complexities of love. The setting, views of mountain life, and the nuances of the story make it appealing.

Drew Thorndike, a botanist from Boston, moves to the Great Smoky Mountains, where he becomes the schoolmaster. He moves into a cabin on the land of the Labans. Here he meets farmer Laban's daughter, Ailanthus ("Lanthy"). He becomes the friend and lover of the young girl who has one leg shorter and smaller than the other. When Drew is called home because of his sister's illness, he does not know that Lanthy is pregnant. Later, he returns to marry her. An appealing and thoroughly detailed love story with sympathetic characterizations.

RISKING LOVE by Doris Orgel. New York: Dial, 1985. Oldest

Dinah Moskowitz, a freshman at Barnard, is madly in love and life seems fine until she is faced with separating from her boyfriend, Gray. When Dinah proposes leaving college and moving to Florida with Gray, her father suggests that she visit a psychiatrist.

The complexities of loving someone and making decisions about that love are exposed through the visits to the therapist. Dinah's ability to relate to Gray in a healthy emotional and physical way is directly related to her feelings about herself and her family relationship. Dinah's passion and desire to follow her young lover wherever he goes are rooted in her feelings of loss which have never been resolved since her parents were divorced. Upon separation, her parents had forced her to choose the parent with whom she would live. When her mother did not fight to keep her, Dinah felt that she had lost her mother's love.

After the sessions with the therapist are completed, Dinah is able to confront her mother about her repressed feelings. She learns that her perceptions of her mother's actions are wrong. Adjusting her perspectives on family love, Dinah is able to return to school and trust in her love for Gray.

This book for young adults could be read by junior high readers, especially since statistics show that some young people are participating in sexual activity at a very young age. The sexual encounters are explicit about the use of birth control. The main character is allowed to confront the uneasy feelings about the use of a diaphragm. On one occasion, Dinah does not play it safe and faces anxious moments when she thinks she might be pregnant.

SHINING STILL by Richard Hawley. New York: Farrar, Straus and Giroux, 1989. Older-Oldest

Teenagers are not supposed to experience love but merely "teenage" or "puppy" love. Nevertheless, real teenagers, like Paul and Juliana do find themselves in love—real love. Without quite realizing how it came to be, Paul and Juliana are transported to a physical and emotional love which renders them inseparable. The pair find the promise of shining futures a nonsequitur to their feelings and their need to be together.

Both sets of parents are distressed about their children's futures. The school guidance counselor, Mr. Lawrence, through whose eyes the story is revealed, comes to know the lovers well. Readers may be surprised at the advice he gives the pair.

The surprising outcome of the book may disturb some readers but the story is dedicated toward showing young teenagers involved in a commitment which goes far beyond infatuation, sexual discovery, and all else except being deeply and irrevocably in love.

SOMEONE TO LOVE ME by Jeannette Eyerly. New York: Lippincott, 1987. Older-Oldest

The reader of this very realistic novel will not miss any of the questions or answers about teenage pregnancy, as the author presents in fairly graphic detail the experience of Patrice.

Patrice, a sophomore in high school, falls in love with Lance, a senior. She knows that Lance has another girl but succumbs to her attraction to him. Naively, she does not protect herself and is pregnant after the first sexual experience. The story follows her through the difficulty of telling her mother, the decision about whether to abort the child, going to a special school for pregnant mothers, the discomforts of pregnancy, and the realities of not being ready for the responsibilities involved. The only elements of happiness are that the baby is born healthy and that Patrice experiences a new kind of love—mother's love.

A WHITE ROMANCE by Virginia Hamilton. New York: Philomel Books, 1987. Oldest

Hamilton, a gutsy writer, attacks a scenario in which interracial friendships and love are involved. When white students begin attending the magnet school in a black neighborhood, Talley surprisingly makes friends with Didi, a white girl. Tally, portrayed as an inexperienced, "good girl" with good grades, is intrigued and titillated by Didi's worldliness. Never having had a loving relationship, she is in awe of Didi's "White Romance" with her drug addict boyfriend, Roady. Enters David, a handsome, calculating drug dealer who shows interest in Talley and she becomes consumed by his charm.

The author painstakingly and painfully portrays a situation of a young girl being sexually awakened while being used by her lover.

PROGRAMMING SUGGESTIONS FOR SECTION I

1. For junior high and young adult classes and discussion groups, assign sections of the book TEENS SPEAK OUT by Jane Rinzler to be read in tandem with fiction titles. In each section of the book, teens discuss such issues as feelings, privacy, family, sex and drugs. If the 1978 edition of SURVIVAL THEMES IN FICTION FOR CHILDREN AND YOUNG PEOPLE is available, use quotes from teens to add to the discussion. TEENS SPEAK OUT can be used with books in other sections of this volume.

2. Encourage children or young people to discuss an issue of choice by assuming the role of characters in a book. Their discussion would be representative of what might be said between these characters about the subject or issue. For example, on the issue of sexual abuse in ABBY MY LOVE, one person would assume the role of Anna, and another Chip. Instead of a discussion, an interview of those assuming the role of characters in a book could be held. Public librarians could tape such interviews and/or discussions and use them for promotion of titles. Copies of tapes could be reproduced for circulation. Interviews and

discussions could vary to include those between a character in the book and the author; 2. between the reader and the author; 3. between two characters in one book; and 4. between the reader and a friend about a book.

3. Classrooms and libraries could provide a "free for all" book sharing time from thirty minutes to an hour. Those participating would freely discuss books read from an assigned list. Groups should be no larger than ten. A leader would be assigned only to monitor the time, so that one person could not monopolize all the time. Otherwise the children or young adults discuss the books in any way they see fit. This avoids the adult approach to the literature. Tapes of such sessions could provide some enlightening information for adults about the young peoples' perceptions of titles, versus those adults expect.

4. Have children or young adults review books from an assigned list to be printed in a newsletter. Prepublished guidelines for the reviews could be given to each prospective writer. If schools or classes are publishing their own newsletters, book reviews could play an important part.

5. For young adult classes or library discussions on parenting, family life, etc., books for younger children could be read and discussed. At issue would be how parents can help young children deal with loneliness, feelings, etc. This same approach could be taken with adult groups. Such reading and discussion would also be appropriate for classes in baby-sitting.

6. Young persons could be taught to do oral history interviews and taping, so as to gain insights about the aged, women, ethnic groups, etc. Public libraries could plan such interviews in relationship to the various celebrations of the year, such as American Indian Month, Black History Month, Woman's History Month, etc. In a public library, oral history could become the focus for an entire year of programming.

7. Teachers and adult leaders who wish to approach book reviewing differently can ask young people to discuss or write about books from the point of view of "The Way the Story Made You Feel" and why. Clues from these reviews could be used for future discussions in the difficult area of feelings.

8. Feelings can also be approached by choosing a scene from the book to reenact. A lot can be learned about thoughts and perceptions when young people are allowed to reenact characters and play out a scene in their own way, using their own language.

9. Have children, classes, discussion groups, scouts, campfire girls, etc. read from assigned lists and prepare original book jackets to be displayed in the library. Reviews could be displayed with the book jackets.

10. Young people could be asked to write letters to a character in a book, after reading from an assigned list. Then another person could be assigned to read the letter and respond as if they were the character.

11. Displays and public relations materials can zero in on some of these sensitive issues as follows:

    a. Display: LITERARY LONERS, Fiction Characters Facing Unusual Challenges. This could also be a booklist.

    b. Provide a centerpiece of a poem or poems dealing with aloneness or loneliness, display books dealing with these issues.

    c. Display: FIVE WAYS TO FIGHT LONELINESS: *Read A Book*—display book jackets or reviews. *Make Something*—display arts and craft titles. *Write or Learn Poetry*—Display appropriate titles. *Learn Photography*—Display appropriate titles. *Keep a Journal*—Display fiction books about characters who kept journals or diaries.

12. Plan and present a Cultural Festival at which children and young people are encouraged and provided time to learn about the dances, music, games, etc. of other cultures. Books of fiction can help with this learning process.

13. Form a Media Production Group made up of children and/or young people. Produce "issue" related films, filmstrips, etc. Have a media expo at the end of the year. Such groups could use the assistance of audio visual personnel, public television facilities, and media companies who often will provide free

equipment or facilities. Segments from the television series, THE POWER OF CHOICE which focused on the problems and dreams of teenagers might be used as an example of what can be produced. These programs focused on various issues including drug abuse, depression, communications, and sex.

14. Form a foster grandparent program at your library so that young people can establish special relationships with the elderly. Elders can lead discussions, help with film programs, etc. Such programs can be arranged through your local Foster Grandparent agency or senior centers.

15. Use biographies of noted figures along with fiction in the presentation of image materials in book talks, displays, etc. This allows the listener to project from the novel to actual people.

16. Select an author to study. Study the way they present characters, plots, actions, resolutions, etc. This allows the student or discussion group to deal with more than the surface of a novel. Such study in public libraries without discussion groups could be provoked by a display which presents one author along with reviews and questions about that author's works.

17. Since one of the major tasks of young children is learning language, words which deal with feelings displayed with appropriate books could be helpful.

18. As an activity for younger children, words could be printed on cards, after discussing the words, children could be asked to take one card and find a book with pictures which represent the feelings on their card. The group of books could be prechosen and scattered on a table.

(SEE SOURCES AND NOTES
FOR MORE PROGRAM SUGGESTIONS)

SELECTED AUDIOVISUALS

A lot of these titles are familiar classics and are listed to show which might be used to improve the approach to the books listed in that category. Most of these titles should be available from educational distributors of video. Many are also available as 16mm films.

For additional media, check listings in Sources and Notes. Materials
from the PBS catalog which can be purchased or rented might be
especially helpful. A regular check for special presentations offered
for children and youth by the major television networks, such as,
After School Specials should be made. Where relevant, titles from
our listing are suggested to use with the films, however, films can also
stand alone as a way of transmitting stories and information.

1. The Individual (Sexuality)
   A CHILD'S INTRODUCTION TO HOW BABIES ARE
   BORN. 30 min. video $19.95 (Youngest) Use with: books for
   the youngest which deal with the new baby in the family. Some
   are listed in the section on families.

2. The Individual (Fears)
   STRONG KIDS, SAFE KIDS. 45 min. video $29.95.
   (Younger) Use with:
   Dark and Full of Secrets by Carrick
   I'll Protect You from the Jungle Beasts by Alexander
   The Night Light by Feder

3. The Individual (Fears, Feelings)
   WHEN PARENTS ARE AWAY. 30 min. video, $19.98
   (Youngest) Use with:
   Sonya's Mommy Works by Alda
   Waiting by Weiss

4. The Individual (Sexuality)
   WHERE DID I COME FROM? 27 min. video, $24.95
   (Younger) Use with:
   The Day We Met by Koehler
   Daniel's Dog by Bogart

5. The Individual (Loners)
   TEX. (S.E. Hinton) 102 min. video, $69.95 (Middle-Older) Use
   with:
   Tex by Hinton
   A Place Between by Newton
   The Best Way Out by Follis
   Last One Home by Osborne

6. The Individual (Loneliness)
   GAL YOUNG UN. 105 min. video, $69.95 (Older) Use with:
   The People Therein by Lee

7. The Individual (Deaf Mute)
   THE HEART IS A LONELY HUNTER. 124 min. $59.95
   (Oldest) Use with:
   Let a River Be by Cummings

8. The Individual (Loneliness, Abuse)
   I KNOW WHY THE CAGED BIRD SINGS. 96 min, $69.95
   (Oldest) Use with:
   Abby My Love by Hadley (Currently being made into a TV film)

9. The Individual (Views of Self and Others)
   TO KILL A MOCKINGBIRD. 129 min., $39.95 (Older-
   Oldest) Use with the book. Also pertinent for young adults
   exploring the politics of racism. (See Religion and Politics)

10. The Individual (Views of Self and Others)
    WHEN THE LEGENDS DIE. 105 min., $29.95 (Older-
    Oldest) Use with the book and
    When Thunders Spoke by Sneve (Reviewed in section 3)

11. The Individual (Views of Self and Others)
    COAL MINER'S DAUGHTER. 124 min., $79.95 (Older-
    Oldest) Use with:
    Come Sing, Jimmy Jo by Paterson

12. The Individual (Views of Self and Others)
    THE JESSE OWENS STORY. 180 min. $69.95 (Middle to
    Oldest) Use with:
    The Runner by Voight

13. The Individual (Views of the Elderly)
    THE GIN GAME. 82 min. $39.95 (Oldest) Use with:
    A Begonia for Miss Applebaum by Zindel (reviewed in section 3)
    and others by Zindel which show teen encounters with the
    elderly such as *Pigman*.

14. The Individual (Views of Self and Others)
    THE AUTOBIOGRAPHY OF MISS JANE PITTMAN. 110
    min. $59.95 (Older-Oldest). Use with the book.

15. The Individual (Views of Self and Others)
    EL NORTE. 141 min. $59.98 (Oldest) Use with:
    Streets of Gold by Branson

16. The Individual (Sexuality)
    HERPES, IT'S NO LAUGHING MATTER. 112 min. $69.95
    (Study Guide) (Oldest) Use with:
    All titles in Sexuality section

17. The Individual (Overcoming Handicaps)
    THE MIRACLE WORKER. 107 min. $59.95 (Middle-Oldest)
    Use with:
    Child of the Morning by Corcoran
    Between Friends by Garrigue

18. The Individual (Views of Self and Others—Farm Life)
    PLACES IN THE HEART. 112 min. $59.98 (Oldest) Use
    with:
    Spud Tackett and the Angel of Doom by Branscum and other
    books by this author. (Reviewed in section 3)
    Carrots and Miggles by Mayhar

19. The Individual (Runaways)
    STREETWISE. 105 min. $59.95 (Older-Oldest) Use with:
    Last One Home by Osborne

20. The Individual (Images of Self and Others)
    PAUL ROBESON. 120 min. $79.95 (Older-Oldest) Use with:
    The Best Way Out by Cheatham
    The Runner by Voight

21. The Individual (Sexuality)
    AIDS UPDATE, PROFILE OF AN EPIDEMIC. 60 min.
    $69.95 (Older-Oldest) Use with:
    Crazy Vanilla by Werbsa
    Night Kites by Kerr

22. The Individual (Alcoholism)
    ALCOHOLISM THE PIT OF DESPAIR. 20 min. $69.95
    (Older-Oldest) Use with:
    The Moonlight Man by Fox

23. The Individual (Feelings)
    EMOTIONS OF LIFE. 63 min. $64.95 (Older)
    Jacob Have I Loved by Paterson
    Turkeylegs Thompson by McCord

24. The Individual (Feelings)
    FREE TO BE YOU AND ME. 45 min. $29.95 (Younger) Use
    with:
    Sonora the Beautiful by Clifton
    Hotel Boy by Kaufman
    That's Not Fair by Fujikawa

25. The Individual (Sexuality)
    THE MIRACLE OF LIFE. 60 min. $39.95 (Older-Oldest) Use
    with:
    First the Egg by Moeri
    Hey Kid! Does She Love Me? by Mazer
    Someone to Love Me by Eyerly

26. The Individual (Sexuality)
    WHAT'S HAPPENING TO ME? 30 min. $19.95 (Older) Use
    with any books in the section on SEXUALITY.

27. The Individual (Views of Others)
    CHILDREN OF A LESSER GOD. 119 min. $79.95 (Older-
    Oldest) Use with: Books portraying the disabled

28. The Individual (Views of Others)
    CHILDREN OF SANCHEZ. 103 min. $59.95 (Older-Oldest)
    Use with:
    And Condors Danced by Snyder

29. The Individual (Sexuality)
    HOW CAN I TELL IF I'M REALLY IN LOVE. 51 min.
    $29.95 (Older-Oldest) Use with:
    Finding David Delores by Willey
    A White Romance by Hamilton
    Shining Still by Hawley

SECTION II
PAIRINGS AND GROUPINGS

Friendship; Peer Pressures; Social Interaction
Families

This text begins by presenting books which place emphasis on the individual, because many experts believe that without successful identity formation, a child approaches learning, interaction and socialization at a deficit. Psychologists and others who study childhood in western societies seem to agree that early in life, children are beginning to build their identities. Erik H. Erikson in discussing a child's delight in taking his or her first steps, states, "This self-esteem grows to be a conviction that one is learning effective steps toward a tangible future, and is developing into a defined self within a social reality. The growing child must, at every step, derive a vitalizing sense of actuality from the awareness that his or her individual way of mastering experience (ego synthesis) is a successful variant of group identity and is in accord with its space-time and life plan."[1] Success in early identity molding is necessary for very young children to function well in the social arenas to which they are later exposed. While learning those rudimentary processes which will provide for progress in the society, such as reading, writing and computing, school-aged children must learn social rules to which they have not been exposed before schooling begins. They must learn the rules of play and the rules of friendship, while also answering the demands of interacting within their most permanent group, the family.

Human development is a complex task, about which expert opinions are too numerous and too controversial to digest in a few sentences, but assuming that there is truth in the aforementioned conclusions, in this section, we proceed to those areas of sociability which most encompass a child's life. Children needing identity reinforcement may experience more fears and anxieties than others at school and in groups. Some may find helpful clues in their identification with book characters, although such correction can't be assumed. Erikson continues, "In this children cannot be fooled by empty praise and condescending encouragement. They may have to accept artificial bolstering of their self-esteem in lieu of something better, but their ego identity gains real strength only from wholehearted and consistent recognition of real accomplishment—i.e., of achievement that has meaning in the culture."[2] However inadvertently, some books for children successfully place emphasis on the progression from reinforced identity to sociability and appear to be psychologically accurate. One example, in reviews to follow, is a book titled, GET LOST LITTLE BROTHER, in which, the main character confronts the conflicts between himself and his older siblings. Todd reinforces his own ego by claiming an island before he can begin to resolve the situation between himself and his brothers. Many of the books included also deal with the establishment and appreciation of rules regarding friendship and group interplay.

Children's fiction, on all levels, indicates that the dominent social institutions affecting children today are those of school and family. While most of the stories are centered around child characters and since many children have few experiences outside of the sphere of these two institutions, it is understandable that so many books have such settings. For some young people, though, religious organizations, various scouting groups, sports teams, and other clubs or routine gatherings become part of the socializing process. It is somewhat harder to find materials which deal with experiences in these other institutional groups, although many stories take place at summer camp. Titles with sports as a theme are available, but the concentration is on male sports. Fewer titles present women in athletics or focus on clubs, gangs, and informal groupings. It can probably be assumed, then, that authors believe that two primary group experiences, school and family, are most important in children's preparation for adolescence, and for their functioning as adults in the larger society.

We recognize adolescence as a special period in life when questioning begins anew. At this time, interaction with peers, adult leaders and family is affected by changing body functions and the impending roles of adulthood. Erikson says, "In their search for a new sense of continuity and sameness adolescents have to refight many of the battles of earlier years, even though to do so they must artificially appoint perfectly well-meaning people to play the role of adversaries, and they are ever ready to install idols, ideals as guardians of a final identity."[3] Thus, many books for adolescents rightfully present young people in conflict with parents and with other adult leaders. While attempting to provide guidance during this period, adult leaders routinely confront in adolescents their questioning of authority, their clannishness in group processes, and their exclusion of those who are different. Therefore, one major flaw in literature for young people may be that options beyond such actions are often not presented. Much of the writing is a literature of sameness, the same school story, the same romance story, or the same parental conflicts, as will become obvious from the repetitive themes in this section's offerings. For those adolescents whose tests of affirmation with their peers fail, and who find themselves frustrated by the group processes surrounding them, what options are there?

Many characterizations of adolescents present egocentric youth flaunting their beliefs and acting more knowledgeable than the adults around them. These books may be psychologically honest, but in many of the best, authors inventively show respect for adult wisdom. Characters whose success results from a struggle for insight are more interesting. A simplistic example of this is the book, TOUGH TIFFANY, which presents a character showing strong ego formations. She is able to solve problems which her parents can't. The author, however, allows Tiffany to be accomplished with assistance from other adults in the community. While condescending to the young person's need to outdo her parents, the credibility of other adults is realized. Recognizing that fictional characterizations which fit psychological and clinical profiles are probably accidental, such writing may reflect an author's sincere effort to portray adolescence in a realistic manner. No matter how self-centered they may be, young people do have questions about their world. With this in mind, books were sought here which place individual adolescents in situations where they encounter negative and positive rules of sociability. Emphasis was placed on characters which showed growth in social graces and/or interaction.

In the section on families, examples of variable patterns of family are included. The different "shapes" of family which are indicative of our present society were readily evident in books for all ages. Reading of todays fiction can help young people to appreciate that the definition of family now encompasses one parent families with either the male or female parent in charge; families with two parents who have been divorced but share the responsibility for the children; families with divorced parents who have remarried; adoptive families; and dysfunctional families. Most difficut to find, were books which present families representing cultural and ethnic variations.

The hope is that in helping children and young people to find these materials, we assist in a small way with the process about which Erikson writes as follows: "Every adult whether he is a follower or a leader, a member of a mass or an elite, was once a child, he was once small. A sense of smallness forms a substratum in his mind, ineradicably. His triumphs will be measured against this smallness, his defeats will substantiate it. The questions as to who is bigger and who can do or not do this or that to whom—these questions fill the adult's inner life far beyond the necessities and the desirabilities which he understands and for which he plans. . . . To assure continuity of tradition, society must early prepare for parenthood in its children . . ."[4]

NOTES

1. Erikson, Erik H. *Childhood and Society,* 2nd ed. New York: W.W. Norton & Co., © 1963, p. 235.
2. Ibid.
3. Ibid, p. 261.
4. Ibid, pp. 404–405.

II. PAIRINGS AND GROUPINGS

Friendship; Peer Pressures; Social Interaction

ALFIE GIVES A HAND by Shirley Hughes. Illus. by the author. New York: Lothrop, Lee and Shepard, 1983. Youngest

The demands of socialization are faced by Alfie when he attends his first birthday party finding another child, as reticent as he, for whom he gives up his security blanket.

AT TAYLOR'S PLACE by Sharon Phillips Denslow. Illus. by Nancy Carpenter. New York: Bradbury, 1990. Youngest

Very young children, as well as adolescents, often find it easier to form their first friendships with the aged, from whom they gain enough self esteem to assist with other relationships. Pastel illustrations emphasize the warmth of the relationship between Tory, a young girl, and her elderly neighbor. The two of them are shown in the workshop where Taylor makes weathervanes.

BATHING UGLY by Rebecca Busselle. New York: Watts (Orchard Books), 1989. Middle-Older

Summer camp is, again, the setting for exposing problems of peer relationships and the pressures which can be imposed on young people in group processes. Thirteen-year-old Betsy Sherman is too plump. While spending a summer at camp, she is selected to receive the "Bathing Ugly Prize." In a first person narrative, readers are allowed to understand Betsy's agonies, while also viewing the ruthlessness of the camp leader, an ex-beauty queen, and Betsy's taunting peers. A surprise ending is provided in which Betsy and her supporters get even. Use with THE GOATS by Brock Cole.

BETWEEN FRIENDS, by Sheila Garrigue. Scarsdale, New York: Bradbury Press, 1978. Middle

When Jill forms a friendship with Dede, who is retarded, she encounters negative reactions from her other friends. Jill is disturbed by this response and by her own mother's hesitancy toward Dede. In spite of everything, Jill maintains her connection with the retarded girl until, finally, her loyalty is tested. Jill promises that she will visit Dede's school on the same day that she has been invited to see her friend Marlene perform in a play. With this dilemma, the author successfully presents a situation where peer pressures conflict with friendship and moral commitment. Jill makes the hard decision to go to Dede's school.

Later, Jill learns that her mother's reason for rejecting Dede was because of fears about her own pregnancy. Being an older parent, her mother faces the possibility of bearing a child with Down syndrome.

Several elements of relationships are dealt with in this book, but the concentration is on friendship. Jill faces the test of loyalty and feels good about her decision. The writing provides enough tension to make the resolution seem real.

BIG BASE HIT by Dean Hughes, (also MAKING THE TEAM). New York: McKay, 1990. Younger

Little Leaguers and others will relate to these companion stories centering on the baseball team. This early group experience can be very traumatic for many young boys and girls, who are faced with a different set of group dynamics than those which they have encountered at play. More often than not, the issues of winning and losing become more acute. Along with the processes of competition, selection and rejection, they may face the insensitivity of adults who become embroiled in the process. In these two simple titles, third grade boys experience the variety of negative and positive feelings wrought by this kind of involvement.

THE BIRTHDAY PARTY by Helen Oxenbury. Illus. by the author. New York: Dial, 1983. Youngest

Several of this author's books deal with the trying circumstances of "firsts" for young children. Among them, are THE DANCING CLASS and THE FIRST DAY AT SCHOOL. This one humorously looks at the preschooler's first birthday party, where a guest is more interested in the presents than in the celebrant.

THE BOY IN THE MOON by Ron Koertge. New York: Little, Brown and Co. (Joy Street Books), 1990. Oldest

This novel for older adolescents presents a fairly typical young romance, but, the characters are well formed. The sexual encounters, awkward but explicit, could be used in discussions on sexuality. The focus is on the relationships between Frieda, Kevin and Nick who have been best friends since the third grade, In their senior year, major changes in their relationships take place. After visiting his mother in California, Kevin returns with a new muscular physique and bleached hair. Nick is both jealous and threatened by Kevin's new look and changed demeanor. The sexual scenes take place while Kevin is absent and Nick and Frieda become intimate. Later, Frieda must choose between going to college and continuing her newly formed relationship with Nick. Each young person faces changes in their individual perspectives as well as the changes among them. Family relationships become a part of the decision making process, when Kevin is determined to break away from the controls of his alchoholic father. This book adequately deals with elements of changing relationships and decision making.

BUDDIES by Barbara Park. New York: Alfred A. Knopf, 1985. Middle-Older

When thirteen-year-old Dinah Feeney goes to camp Miniwawa, she is determined to change her life and become popular. She finds herself stuck with Fern Wadley, "the Nerd," although she prefers to spend her time with two popular girls, Cassandra and Marilyn. Dinah silences her conscience and participates in a mean caper which hurts Fern terribly.

Examined here is the child's need to belong. In the end Dinah faces feelings of guilt and responsibility and she learns about the real meaning of friendship.

THE COMING HOME CAFE by Gayle Pearson. New York: Atheneum, 1988. Oldest

Associations and friendships form for many reasons—by chance, and out of need. In this novel, an unlikely association between three people seeking work during the depression is formed by chance. Elizabeth has joined Eddie traveling on freight trains to find work. These two meet Lenora, a young Black woman. Reluctantly at first, they travel together, work together in the fields, and eventually settle for a while in the abandoned "Coming Home Cafe" in Jacksonville.

Through the events which have caused Elizabeth to leave home in an attempt to save her family, the happenings on the road, and the conversations between the three travelers, readers are offered a suspenseful picture of survival during the depression years. The struggle to find work, and the hardships on the road will also help young people understand the plight of todays homeless families. A glimpse of racial prejudice during those times is visible through the characterization of Lenora. This title could be used with others on the homeless and the depression years.

CRICKET AND THE CRACKERBOX KID by Alane Ferguson. New York: Bradbury, 1990. Middle

This author offers a fresh approach to the intricacies of friendship. Cricket Winslow, is lonely and would like to own a dog. She finds "Treasure" at the dog pound. Eventually, Cricket also finds a friend at school, a boy named Dominic from the other side of town. The trouble begins when Dominic meets the dog and recognizes it is his own lost dog. The resulting scenes which include a classroom trial to settle the matter, will emotionally involve children in the final solution.

THE CYBIL WAR by Betsy Byars. Illus. by Gail Owens. New York: Viking, 1981. Middle-Older

Simon has a crush on Cybil Ackerman until she steals his role in the the school play. He wants to get even, and enlists the aid of his friend Toney. Cybil Ackerman becomes the catalyst for Simon's recognition that he has been used, and that Toney is less than a true friend.

Since they were small, Simon and Toney have remained friends inspite of the fact that Toney tells half-truths, allowing Simon to be blamed for his mistakes. Simon finally realizes that he must protect himself from being the butt of Toney's lies. These issues of friendship are explored in a very humorous narrative.

DEADLY STRANGER by Peg Kehret. New York: Dodd, Mead and Company, 1987. Middle-Older

Concerns about friendship are couched in this mystery story. Just when twelve-year-old Katie Osborne, starts at her new school and meets a possible friend, Shannon Lindstrom, Shannon disappears. Pursuing their relationship, leads to Katie being stalked by Shannon's kidnapper.

Using the popular style of speaking first from Katie's point of view, and then from Shannon's the author builds a suspenseful mystery, while presenting elements of the adolescent girls' lives and relationships.

EATING CROW by Lila Hopkins. New York: Franklin Watts, 1988. Middle-Older

No matter how unlikely it might seem that a mute Jewish boy would arrive at an all Black school, or that this child would own a talking crow, this background provides for a zany celebration of friendship between two boys who are different. Add to this the character of Old Miss Sophie, who everybody knows is an oddball and who the kids believe may be a root doctor or conjure woman, and readers are hooked.

Croaker Douglas is asked by his teacher to "eat crow" and make friends with Zeke, who lost his voice from the trauma of losing his mother and father in an airplane accident. Zeke has come to live with an aunt in a small town in North Carolina where he is placed in the same classroom with Croaker. Fascinated by Zeke's circumstance and even more intrigued by his pet talking crow it is easy for Croaker to get over his first feelings of hostility toward the white intruder. Thus, the tentative frienship begins. The happenings which surround the evolving friendship, are entertaining, sure to capture the interest of the most reluctant reader. In one irresistable scene, when the boys have gone fishing together, Croaker's Labrador retriever and the crow fight over a fish caught by the two boys. The truce between the two pets is symbolic of the growing friendship between Croaker and Zeke. Their relationship is sealed when they both confront local bullies, first with Croaker saving the day and then with Zeke regaining his voice to save Croaker.

THE FASTEST FRIEND IN THE WEST by Vicki Grove. New York: Putnam, 1990. Older-Oldest

Seventh grader, Lori, is overweight, shy, lonely and friendless. The depth of her loneliness is symbolized by the fact that she paints her room such a dark blue that it appears to be black. Lori loses herself in fantasy until the day that she meets Vernita who is homeless. Lori tells her story in the first part of the narrative and in the second part Vernita speaks. While Lori is experiencing feelings of rejection, Vernita's lonelines is caused by the fact that her family is homeless and has moved from place to place for the last few years. The two form a strong friendship based on their mutual needs, their understanding of each other, and their mutual insights into loneliness. Lori gains strength and Venita has to move on. This is an important book because of it's special look at relationships which form between unlikely associates out of need. Elements of homelessness are present through the characterization of Vernita, but this subject is not dealt with as realistically as in other titles. The strength of this book is in the author's depiction of adolescents in crisis—rising above it through friendship.

FIRST GRADE TAKES A TEST by Miriam Cohen. Illus. by Lillian Hoban. New York: Greenwillow, 1980. Younger

Adjustment to the group process of school and the negative fallout from competition, are evident in this story about a young girl who moves into a first grade class for the gifted.

THE FLUNKING OF JOSHUA T. BATES by Susan Richards Shreve. Illus. by Diane de Groat. New York: Alfred A. Knopf, 1984. Younger

Few titles deal with the subject of repeating a grade in school. This one presents a rather straightforward and realistic portrayal of a child repeating third grade. Conversations between Joshua and his teacher reveal some of the issues involved.

FRIENDS FIRST by Christine McDonnell. New York: Viking, 1990. Older

In another story about young friends whose relationships change when they enter adolescence, Miranda and Gus deal with the usual adolescent angst placing pressures on their friendship. Complicating the situation, Miranda experiences a near rape by neighborhood thugs. With the help of her sensitive mother, Miranda gradually overcomes her trauma regarding the violent encounter and is able to move closer to Gus. The awkwardness of developments between the adolescents seems real but many of the issues introduced like the near rape are not dealt with in depth.

GET LOST LITTLE BROTHER by C.S. Adler. New York: Clarion Books (Ticknor and Fields of Houghton Mifflin), 1983. Middle

The rivalries between brothers are portrayed to their extremes in this story. Todd is tormented by and feels powerless against his older twin brothers. They leave him locked in the bathroom all day and then threaten revenge if he tells his parents.

Although the problems faced by Todd are those of family, the story has been included in this section because the greatest peer pressures can come from siblings and because of the friendship between Todd and a strong young female.

Louie LeVoy is Todd's colorful friend who helps him to devise a plan to claim a nearby island as his own. This claim becomes the reason for a better relationship between Todd and his brothers. Although the parents in this story emerge as less than adequate, the relationship between the brothers is boldly detailed.

GOWIE CORBY PLAYS CHICKEN by Gene Kemp. London: Faber and Faber, 1979. Middle

An English father remembers how a school relationship may have saved him from a life of brutality and crime, in this story styled as a flashback.

Gowie Corby hated school and got along with no one. He fought and intimidated the children in his class, especially Jonathan and Heather. He made frequent trips to the principal's office and was excused only because the principal realized that Gowie's anger resulted from his home situation.

Gowie's father was in jail and his brother was in reform school. His mom did the best that she could, working hard day and night. It was not until Rosie came to live next door that Gowie began to show improvement. Rosie eased herself into Gowie's life and helped him to improve his behavior. On occasion, he still found pleasure in tormenting Heather, but overall things were better until his brother came home from reform school.

His brother, Mark, threatened to kill all of Gowie's pet rats, if he continued to keep company with Rosie. (Until this point, the fact that Rosie is Black has not been an issue). Mark later rescinded his ultimatum when Rosie saved him and a friend from returning to reform school for breaking parole.

This is primarily a story about a troubled child. It offers an example of a friend becoming the catalyst for such a child to move in a more positive direction. The fact that Rosie's race is not mentioned until the end may have been intended to show that this was inconsequencial to Gowie. Presenting the issue near the end of the story, and allowing a quick resolution may have reflected the author's inability to handle the details needed for such a resolution, or the author may have intended to show that Mark's negative attitudes toward Rosie were territorial rather than racial.

In the postlogue it is learned that Gowie married Heather and that Rosie went on to be a Nobel Prize winning doctor.

THE GREAT MALE CONSPIRACY by Betty Bates. New York: Holiday House, 1986. Middle-Older

What begins like an average story of school age shenanigans turns out to be a narrative which presents unusual glimpses of mature relationships. Maggie struggles with her own feelings about males as she views and is involved in the dissolution of her sister's marriage. Maggie feels sorry for her sister when she is left, by her con-man husband, with a new baby and no money. Maggie is especially disturbed because she was also enchanted by the deserter's charm. In addition, Maggie has a negative view of her father who is involved in research and according to Maggie, "seems as if he's on his own planet." With these views heavy in her heart, Maggie can no longer tolerate the clowning of her friend and classmate, Todd. She hopes that her sister, her mother, and all women will realize that a male conspiracy operates against females.

Maggie is even more distressed when Burl, the con-man, calls her sister Alicia, asking for money, and when she discovers that Alicia is seeing another man. Gradually, Maggie begins to understand that she cannot compare Alicia's new beau to the wayward Burl. She also has a chance to realize that her father has a lot more gumption than she thought. With sane and thorough characterizations, and with humor, the author offers the reader substantative material about choices and decisions. Maggie's adjustment seems honest.

HATING ALISON ASHLEY by Robin Klein. New York: Viking Kestrel, 1987. Middle

The painful process of building a friendship is seen in this story of Ericka Yurken, dubbed "Yuk" by her classmates. Erica is proud to be one of the smartest students at Barringa East Primary School, that is, until Alison Ashley arrives.

Alision is beautiful, rich, neat, and smart. Erica views her with feelings of envy bordering on hate. Her sometimes humorous efforts to outdo Alison all fall flat.

The author deftly exposes Erica's feelings of competition, while gradually building sympathy for Alison who is privileged but lonely. The contrasting views of the two girls' homes help the reader to view the circumstances of the two. Erica's home is old, cluttered, and filled with noise and activity, while Alison's is modern and neat to a fault.

The annual school camp is the frequently used vehicle selected by this author to bring the two reluctant friends together. Erica, who has visions of being a grand actress writes the camp play and expects to be the star, but experiences stage fright. Alison is the one who at the end calls for the author and gives Erica her moment of glory, from this point, the friendship is established.

HENRY'S HAPPY BIRTHDAY by Holly Keller. Illus. by the author. New York: Greenwillow, 1990. Youngest

Another view of the trauma suffered by the young in anticipation of one of the most important early social events—a birthday party. Henry anticpates disaster at his upcoming birthday party, but on that day, everything proceeds normally. Black and white illustrations help to amplify the emotions felt by Henry.

I'M CALLING MOLLY by Jane Kurtz. Illus. by Irene Trivas. Albert Whitman, 1990. Youngest

Four-year old Christopher is pleased to have learned his friend Molly's phone number. When he dials, Molly is always busy with some other friend and promises to return his call. Christopher experiences feelings of rejection because Margie waits for her other friends to leave before returning his calls. The book illustrates an interracial friendship, but the theme is universal. Accurately portrayed are the sporatic nature of very young friendships and the ease of healing relationships at this age.

IS IT THEM OR IS IT ME? by Susan Haven. New York: Putnam, 1990. Older

When Molly enters high school, she is self conscious about her body and the way she laughs. Her best friend, Kathy, has entered a private school and is not present to offer support. Molly longs for

Kathy and for a more voluptuous body. This typical school story deals with peer pressures, school adjustment, family crisis, and the desire for acceptance. The writing is a little better than average, and the combined school and family events strengthen the overall presentation.

JANET HAMM NEEDS A DATE FOR THE DANCE by Eve Bunting. Boston: Clarion Books, 1986. Middle-Older

The story centers on the familiar theme of seventh-graders seeking a date for the dance. Inadvertently, Janet finds herself involved in a lie, when she announces that she has a date for the dance and her friends make assumptions about who it might be. Briefly, the reader views Janet's crush on an older friend of her brother. She hopes that with her brother's help she can entice his friend to take her to the dance. When all fails, Janet more closely observes her own friend, Rolf, whom she ignored previously as a possible date.

This is a slight and popular approach to the subject of friendship, crushes, peers and lying.

JERRY ON THE LINE by Brenda Seabrooke. New York: Bradbury, 1990. Middle.

Jerry, a fourth grader, has learned how to survive very well as a latchkey child. Then one day, he receives a phone call from second-grader Sherita, who is also a latchkey child but feels alone and afraid. The story follows Jerry's growing concern and involvement in Sherita's plight, against the background of his involvement in sports. Jerry shows considerable individual growth in his concern for others in this simple fast-paced story.

JUST FRIENDS by Norma Klein New York: Alfred A. Knopf, 1990. Older-Oldest

This title could be considered for discussions of and listings of fiction relating to sexuality, but strong elements of characterizations and conversations have to do with relationships and their meaning. Isabel and Stuart have been good friends since nursery school. During their senior year, Isabel would like to have Stuart as a boyfriend. Stuart instead likes Ketti. Isabel turns to Gregory as second choice. Gregory is a rather stereotypical intellectual outcast, who likes poetry. Adult characters are in the picture and issues of sexuality including lesbianism are dealt with, but the value of this title is in the questions about relationships presented by the interaction of the characters.

LIBBY ON WEDNESDAY by Zilpha Keatly Snyder. New York: Doubleday, 1990. Middle-Older

The pros and cons of home education do not often appear in children's books. In this title, the characterization of Libby is formed by the fact that until the story begins, she has been educated at home. Her mother has now decided that Libby should attend public school. Libby enters school, feeling that she is much superior in intelligence to her fellow students. The students, in turn, look upon Libby as a snob. Libby, who has previously kept a journal, joins a writing club where she finds friendship.

The story is much more complex than it initially appears. Libby's family and other members of the family are presented as being loving but obviously ouside of the norm. Libby, in some ways, is indeed a snob, but has childish needs. Her socialization process has been thwarted by her isolation. Several members of the writing club have their own problems and handicaps. Through Libby's journal, the reader has a view of the feelings and thoughts of the central character while the narrative carries on the action. The writings of other members in the writing club reveal the sometimes serious problems which they face, including child abuse. With these many ingredients, the messages, still, do not seem heavy handed. Probably because of the interjection of humor and the skillful structure of the writing, the story remains well-balanced.

LOVE FROM THE FIFTH GRADE CELEBRITY by Patricia Reilly Giff. Illus. by Leslie Morrill. New York: Delacorte, 1986. Middle

While spending the summer together in the country, Casey Valentine and Tracy Matson become great friends. They have many adventures together and it doesn't matter that Tracy can't read.

Casey returns home ready for school and expecting to be elected the class president when, by chance, Tracy's father gets a job nearby. Tracy moves to town and enters Casey's class. At first, Casey is elated, but, she soon becomes disturbed by Tracy's growing popularity. Tracy ingratiates herself with her new classmates (sometimes at Casey's expense), hiding her inability to read. Worst of all, Tracy gets elected as class president. In anger and

distress, Casey reveals the embarrassing secret that Tracy can't read.
This story explores the meaning of friendship and the emotions of jealousy and competitiveness. Both girls grow and learn from the resolution of their conflict and remain friends.

MAKE FRIENDS, ZACHERY! by Muriel Blaustein. Illus. by the author. New York: HarperCollins, 1990. Youngest

Zachery always has fun with his parents and does not like it when thay go out without him. To wean Zachery away from their company, Mr. and Mrs. Tiger invite cousin Alfie to go along on a camping trip. Both little Tigers are used to having their own way. When they meet with trouble, the two help each other and realize the benefit of having friends. The illustrations are charming and children will identify with the little Tigers representing themselves.

MAXIE, ROSIE, AND EARL—PARTNERS IN GRIME by Barbara Park. Illus. by Alexander Strogart. New York: Alfred A. Knopf, 1990. Younger-Middle

By chance, three elementary school misfits become friends. While waiting to be disciplined, Maxie, Rosie, and Earl decide to leave school together. A fire drill interrupts their escape and the three hide in the trash dumpster. Thus, they become partners in "grime." Before managing to make their final exit, they are seen by the school janitor. The partners realize that, when they return to school on Monday, their caper will be exposed. Children will relate to the plight of the three cohorts in this story, and "What would you do?" discussions could result from the reading.

THE METHOD by Paul Robert Walker. New York: Harcourt Brace Jovanovich (Gulliver), 1990. Older

Centering on the main character, Albie, the author offers another story of adolescent sexual awakening, peer pressures and group interaction. Discontented Albie has always wanted to be an actor. When Mrs. Pierce, the drama teacher, begins a summer institute for budding actors, Albie auditions and is selected for the training program. The remainder of the story revolves around the group dynamics which slowly evolve during the institute. The device of placing a small group of adolescents in an isolated setting to detail problems of interaction is not new. It was used by

Scoppotone in her controversial title concerning homosexuality, TRYING HARD TO HEAR YOU. The device works well here. Albie discovers things about himself and about his peers as he watches and participates in the drama outside of the classroom. He is smitten with one girl but has to settle for second best. When he attempts a sexual encounter, Albie encounters some surprises. The story is somewhat slow moving but the intricacies of the developing relationships are interesting enough to keep readers captivated and the author has designed a very real character in Albie Jensen.

THE MISSING TOOTH by Joanna Cole Illus. by Marilyn Hafner. New York: Random House (Step Into Reading Books), 1988. Younger

For the youngest readers, the author presents best friends, Robby and Arlo, who are so close they dress alike and do most of the same things. Their friendship is threatened when wagers are offered about who will be the first to lose the next tooth. Humorous illustrations match the humor in the story.

MORE THAN MEETS THE EYE by Jeanne Betancourt. New York: Bantam, 1990. Older-Oldest

Although this title intoduces very real issues of interracial relationships and the plight of Cambodians adjusting to American life, the story's eventual resolution is less than satisfying. During her sophomore year in high school, Liz Gaynor has accepted the assignment of introducing Dary, a Cambodian girl to the school's routines. Dary grapples with learning English and adjusting to American "teen" culture. Through her character, readers gain insight to the difficulties faced by immigrant youth. The interracial problems arise when Liz starts dating Ben Lee, a Chinese-American student. Ben and Liz must face the prejudices of their parents and their peers. It is the characterization of Brad which is most problematic. He has a crush on Liz and is portrayed as being virulently racist, but changes his mind in the end. Appropriate reasons, actions and thoughts are not provided to prepare the reader for this sudden change. The story, otherwise, is interestingly told and the subject matter is important.

MRS. ABERCORN AND THE BUNCE BOYS, by Liza Fosburgh. New York: Four Winds Press, 1986. Middle-Older

After their father's death, the Bunce boys (Otis and Will), move to a new town with their mother. Accompanying them is their mother's new, hot-tempered boyfriend. Otis and Will stick together and soon become friends with their new neighbor, Mrs. Abercorn. She loans them books, takes them fishing, and gives Will driving lessons.

When the boys are ready to return to Ohio, they realize that the old lady will miss them. Understanding that she will need company, they decide to leave a dog, which they have grown to love, with Mrs. Abercorn.

This could be considered a story about disfunctional families, because of the mother's boyfriend who despite living with them does not relate well to the children. But, most of all the focus is on the formation of friendship between young and old—each with their special needs.

MY FRIEND JACOB by Lucille Clifton. Illus. by Thomas Digrazia. New York: Dutton, 1980. Younger

This book on friendship shows the special interaction between a young Black boy and his adolescent friend and neighbor, who is Caucasian and mildly retarded.

MY OWN PRIVATE SKY by Delores Beckman. New York: Dutton, 1980. Middle-Older

Friendship between the young and the very old, is dealt with here with unusual poignancy.

OFFBEAT FRIENDS, by Elfie Donnelly. Trans. by Anthea Bell. New York: Crown, 1982. Middle

From the time that she meets Mrs. Panachek on a park bench, eleven-year-old Mari is intrigued by the eighty-year-old woman. Mrs. Panachek wears one red and one black sock, and tells Mari that the red one is warmer than the black one. Mari also listens to the woman's tales of woe, in which, her stepson is blamed for her current situation and for forcing her out of business.

Mari tries to save Mrs. Panachek from her circumstance as an inmate at a nearby mental hospital, Alden Yards. When Mari brings the old lady to her home, her parents show unusual patience and tolerance. They sympathize with Mari's feelings but insist that the woman must be returned to the hospital. When they return, Mari learns that the hospital is not as bad as she had envisioned. She vows to visit Mrs. Panachek regularly.

One of the most humorous scenes in the book takes place when Mrs. Panachek is having dinner at Mari's house. Mari's grandmother, a stickler for decorum, is frustrated when the whole family eats with their hands, like Mrs. Panachek. This is a humorous story about friendship between the young and the old. The issue of mental illness is introduced and although not dealt with in depth, could become the focus of discussion from reading this story.

ON MY HONOR by Marion Dane Bauer. New York: Houghton Mifflin (Clarion Books), 1986. Middle-Older

This ninety page story portrays the ultimate negative result from submission to the wishes of a dominant peer. From the beginning, Joel wants to spend the day at the swimming pool, but can't find a way to disagree with the wishes of his friend Tony, who usually has his way. When challenged by Tony to swim in the polluted and treacherous local river, Joel again succumbs. Too late, he realizes that Tony can't swim, and Joel's attempts to rescue his friend are fruitless. This book could be used with others in the section on Celebration of Life and Death, but although Jeff's guilt and sorrow are major factors, the lessons about being led by others are also strong.

THE OVER THE HILL WITCH by Ruth Calif. Illus. by Joan Holub. Gretna, Louisiana: Pelican, 1990. Middle

Almost every location has a town witch, usually an old woman, who lives alone. After his father dies in a tractor accident, ten-year-old, Gary Benson, moves with his mother from their farm to a nearby town in the Osarks. Gary joins the local boys in a prank to frighten the old woman, known as the witch. When caught, Gary is punished by having to work for the old woman. Superstition and prejudice surface in the adults when other boys involved in the caper become ill. Meantime, Gary has grown to like the old woman, and has to make choices about his future relationships.

One tires of old women being characterized as witches, but in this story at least the error of that designation is dealt with in detail.

PICKING UP THE PIECES. by Betty Bates. New York: Holiday House, 1981. Older

In a more than adequate story focusing on girl-boy relation-ships, at school, Dexter Mead and Nell Beaumont are "second stringers"—"ordinary plodding types." Nell considers her relation-ship with Dexter as ongoing until a "first string girl" named Lacey takes a fancy for the outstanding athelete. Nell watches Dexter's entrance into the the "first string" crowd, and the reader is offered a view of peer influences affecting changes in behavior. Dexter begins to drink and to carouse with friends of Lacey's. Lacey is self-centered and is obviously using Dexter. It is she who causes a car accident in which Dexter is injured. The leg injury means that Dexter can no longer participate in sports.

At first, Nell retains feelings of resentment and does not attempt to reestablish her friendship with Dexter. But eventu-ally, she nobly decides to help with Dexter's adjustment to his handicap.

RACHEL VELLARS, HOW COULD YOU? by Lois I. Fisher. New York: Dodd, Mead and Company, 1984. Middle-Older

What could have been just another popular story about girls and school, presents views of friendship, peers and of family. The characters of Rachel and Cory are well delineated so that the conflicts which evolve between the two and Cory's resulting frustrations about Rachel are believable.

Rachel Vellars and Cory, both sixth graders are best friends. They live in the same apartment building and have in common the fact that their mothers don't live with them. Cory lives alone with her father and Rachel lives with her father and his various lady friends.

Beth Lowry enters the picture when Cory offers comfort upon the loss of Beth's pet cat. When Cory begins to consort with a new group of friends, she encounters Rachel's jealousy. Pleased with her new friendships, Cory resents Rachel's interference and rejects her. Later, Cory uncovers the shallowness in some of her new friends and reestablishes her friendship with Rachel. Together the two triumph by winning a kite-making contest.

RISKS AND ROSES by Jan Slepian. New York: Philomel, 1990. Middle-Older

Authors offer children a limited number of titles which present the possible viciousness which can arise in female clubs and gangs. In this simple straighforward story, those possibilities are explored through the action and excellent characterizations. Eleven-year-old Skip has just moved to a new city neighborhood. She is pleased when allowed to be part of the local gang. When the girls form a secret club, the ruthlessness of the gang leader, Jean Persico, becomes obvious as each member must meet a dare designed by Jean. Skip becomes disenchanted with the group when her sister Angela is forced to cut the blooms from old Mr. Kaminsky's prize roses. The old man has commanded Skip's respect because he treats her retarded sister, Angela, kindly. Skip makes the hard decision to confront Persico and leave the group.

THE RUNAWAYS by Ruth Thomas New York: Lippincott, 1989. Middle-Older

The circumstances which bring Julia and Nathan together are unlikely but make interesting reading. The two outcasts find a stash of money in an abandoned house. After exposing their wealth at school, the two decide to run away together so as not to be discovered by the authorities. The interracial, scraggly pair become good friends and learn a lot about survival as runaways. Good reading.

SALTED LEMONS by Doris Buchanan Smith. New York: Four Winds Press, 1980. Middle-Older

During World War II, Darby Bannister has just moved with her family and faces adjustment to a new neighborhood and a different way of life in Atlanta, Georgia. Having moved south from Washington, D.C., Darby soon finds that she is considered a Yankee, in spite of her perception that the Mason Dixon Line represents the division between north and south. Darby's first friend is Yoko, who is Japanese and a native of Atlanta. Darby is happy to have a friend but finds life even more complicated when the neighborhood children call her "Jap" lover; and when they accuse the kind owner of a store nearby of being a spy because of his foreign accent.

Elements of the war and the eventual displacement of Yoko and her family to Japanese interment camps make this story worthwhile for discussions of that period, but the majority of the story deals with Darby's struggle to understand a new community and to be accepted. Strong religious elements are present with scenes detailing Darby's reading of the Bible and her attendance at Sunday school.

SAM AND THE MOON QUEEN by Alison Cragin Herzig and Lawrence Mali. New York: Clarion, 1990. Middle-Older

Readers view the plight of the homeless through Sam's discovery of a young girl and her dog in the basement of his apartment building. Sam is thirteen and lives with his mother and her friend, a waitress. Sam befriends the young girl and calls her "December" when she refuses to reveal her name. Through his guided tours of the city, led by December, Sam learns about the process of survival on the streets. The book is well written, with good descriptions, and good characterizations.

THE SEASON OF SECRET WISHES by Iva Prochazkova. Translated by Elizabeth D. Crawford. New York: Lothrop, Lee and Shepard, 1989. Older

Friendship and family in a different part of the world are viewed in this story which begins with young Kapka exploring her new home in Prague. From her room, she can climb out on the roof and see the city.

Colorful characters are introduced although in not much depth. A curious old lady with a mink coat in her closet, lives downstairs. Papa, an artist, retreats to bed when the authorities will not allow him to display his art works. In this setting where ideas are controlled by the State, Kapka finds a friend in Radek, whose father is an alcoholic. With Radek's help, and with the assistance of a community of artists, a showing of Papa's art is arranged at a local site, only the authorities intervene again.

Something seems to be missing from this novel, although the characters of Kapka and Radek are well done. The political view of a restrictive society is not made clear. All the reader knows is that for some reason the authorities intervene. These problems could be due to the translation. The strongest part of the book is the growing relationship between Kapka and Radek. Scenes of Prague are offered through Kapka's eyes.

THE SHADOW BROTHERS by A.E. Cannon. New York, Doubleday, 1990. Older

A special account of relationships and the pressures which can affect them is offered for older readers. Identity struggles intrude upon the relationship between Marcus Jenkins and his foster brother, Henry. Henry is a Navajo Indian, the son of a friend of Marcus's father. Henry has lived with the Jenkins family since he was seven and his mother died. It is during their Junior year, that a newcomer at school, an Ute Indian, arouses anxieties in Henry about his ethnicity.

Although some aspects of the relationship are believable and the pain experienced by Marcus observing the changes in Henry, seems real, it does seem unusual that the question of heritage has never surfaced before this. It also seems unlikely that Henry has not had more contact with his Indian family before these pressures arise. The story could spark enough interest among older teens to produce some interesting and worthwhile discussion, including changing Mormon attitudes toward American Indians. Marcus's family is identified as being Mormon.

TAKE A CHANCE GRAMPS by Joy Davies Okimoto. Little, Brown and Co. (Joy Street Books), 1990. Middle-Older

Although slight, this is a worthwhile story of commiseration between the young and old. Janie feels lost without her best friend who has moved away and gramps, who is widowed, is suffering from depression. Together they find a way out of their doldrums. Useful for its view of adolescents relating to the aged.

THANK YOU, DOCTOR MARTIN LUTHER KING, JR.! by Eleanora E. Tate. New York: Watts, 1990. Middle

After being bombarded with white images on television and elsewhere, many Black children enter school with low self images and confused ideas of beauty. This story attacks the problem directly although with less didacticism than it might. When Gumbo Grove Elementary school prepares a President's month play, Mary Elouise who is Black doesn't relish her role as narrator of the Black History section. She does not want to be different from her white peer and role model, Brandy. Grandmother and a Black storyteller are the adults who help Mary Elouise improve her self image and learn about her heritage. The message is obvious, but needed, and should be used for discussions of racial prejudices. This title could also be extremely helpful in parenting classes.

THEY'RE ALL NAMED WILDFIRE by Nancy Springer. New York: Atheneum, 1989. Middle

Using an appealing vehicle to introduce issues of prejudice and racism, the story is told by Jenny, who notes the arrival of

Shanterey Lucas in her rural Pennsylvania neighborhood. Peer pressures are applied when school friends taunt Shanterey, while Jenny tries to befriend the Black girl. Both girls like horses and Shantery owns a collection of model horses. When the girls meet a neighbor's palomino horse, they name it Wildfire, after Shantery's collection. As the friendship develops, the author intensifies the atmosphere of hatred around the two. Jenny succumbs to community pressure and joins in threats against the Lucas family. In the frey, Wildfire is killed and the Lucas family is forced to move. There are no pat solutions offered here, but Jenny admits guilt about her part in the harrassment of the family. The characterizations are good and the exploding fuse of hatred shown developing is gripping. Children are allowed to make up there minds about much that is right or wrong in this situation.

TODAY FIFTH GRADE TOMORROW THE WORLD by Candice F. Ransom. Illus. by Estella Lee Hickman. New York: Willowisp Press, 1989. Middle

Many preteens search continually for books which deal with the difficulties of becoming one of the crowd or the "in group." In this one, like others, Aubrey Shannon, ten years old lies for approval. She tells everyone that her mother is an actress and her father is a football star. How hard it is to maintain a lie, and how relationships can be formed without lies, are the messages.

WHERE HAVE ALL THE TIGERS GONE? by Lynn Hall. New York: Scribner's, 1989. Older-Oldest

The vehicle is different but the message is the same. Fifty year old, Jo Herne, relives her adolescent years as she flies home to Iowa for her high school class reunion. Like many of today's teens, during those years, Jo felt like and outsider. She remembers her old associates and the pain of seeking acceptance. Through her thoughts, a real teenager emerges. The approach is somewhat sentimental, but might help some readers realize that adults in their lives were once teenagers.

WHOSE SIDE ARE YOU ON? by Emily Moore. New York: Farrar, Straus and Giroux, 1988. Middle-Older

In a moment of anger after failing math, Barbara throws away her report card. She tries to retrieve it, but the garbage truck drives away with the trash. When her teacher suggests that she must have a tutor in math, Barbara reluctantly agrees.

Barbara lives in the same building with her classmate and "pest," TJ. and she is distressed when she discovers that her assigned tutor is one and the same. After the tutoring begins, she soon learns that TJ is not only smart, but also patient and likeable.

When TJ suddenly disappears, Barbara sets out to find him. She blames his grandfather for the disappearance. After picketing in front of the grandfather's apartment, Barbara learns that she does not realize all the facts. Her lone supporter has been Kim, an outcast from the "in group" at school.

This is a story which looks at the strange shades of friendship, and provides insight to the tenuous nature of relationships built on false principles. Barbara learns to like TJ, and finds out that Kim is really okay. When Kim becomes her friend, Barbara becomes the rejected one. The picketing situation seems a little contrived and sensational. Transitions are not always smooth, but the author successfully provides enough suspense to keep the reader involved.

THE WONDER SHOES by Eva Bernatova. Illus. by Fiona Moodie. Farrar, Straus and Giroux, 1990. Younger

When a circus comes to town, Emma meets a dancer who teaches her to pirouette and gives her a pair of red dancing shoes. Being new in town, Emma has been lonely and wants nothing more than to be accepted by the local children. She tries to make an impression on them with her dancing, but it is only when she joins the others in forming their own circus, that Emma is welcomed.

II. PAIRINGS AND GROUPINGS

Families

THE ADVENTURES OF JOHNNY MAY by Robbie Branscum. Illus. by Deborah Howland. New York: HarperCollins, 1984. Middle

This author has written several books which give young people a strong sense of life and circumstance in the Arkansas hills. In this story, Johnny May tries to make Christmas pleasant for her grandparents. A simple view of family life, poverty, and celebration in the hill country is presented. A later story titled JOHNNY MAY GROWS UP concentrates on Johnny May and a love interest but still retains a strong sense of place.

ALICE IN RAPTURE, SORT OF by Phyllis Reynolds Naylor. Atheneum, 1989. Middle-Older

What appears, at first, to be just another pre-teen story of growing up and adolescent love, presents substantially more. Although the focus is on the boy-girl aspect of Alice's life, the reader also gets a glimpse of a one parent family headed by a father. Since Alice's mom has died, Alice's need for a female with whom she can relate and from whom she can seek advice is also revealed as the story progresses. The plot is different from many others which deal with first love and the first kiss, because it humorously presents some of the social questions related to singular dating. Alice, for one, decides that she is not ready for the demands of having a "steady" when she is just entering junior high. She and "boyfriend" Patrick agree to be just close friends for awhile. This book is preceeded by THE AGONY OF ALICE. The socialization aspects of this book are important enough to consider its use with others in the Friendship; Peer Pressures; Social Interaction section. The two titles used together present an interesting picture of family told with contagious humor.

THE AMAZING MEMORY OF HARVEY BEAN by Molly Cone. Illus. by Robert MacLean. New York: Houghton Mifflin, 1980. Middle

Harvey, disturbed by the impending separation of his parents, meets Mr. and Mrs. Katz, and Mrs. Katz teaches Harvey her system for remembering things. Gaining this new skill ameliorates the boy's feelings about his parents.

AND CONDORS DANCED by Zilpha Keatly Snyder. New York: Delacorte Press, 1987. Middle-Older

In this story, set in historical California, Carly is the youngest in the family. Against the backdrop of a mother, who feigns illness to escape responsibility; older brothers and sisters succumbing to the will of a stern father and demanding mother; and Carly's sources of comfort and joy, Aunt Mehitabel, and her Chinese servant, Woo Ling, Carly's story revolves. While the author focuses on Carly's situation, in scenes about her dog being attacked by a coyote, and about her warm interchanges with Aunt M. and Woo Ling, a flat but more detailed painting of family and place emerges in the plot. Revealed are quarrels over water in the area, the story of Peter, Carly's brother who died before she was born, her mother's retreat based on her inability to accept life in the West, and more. The complexities of family life are obviously present in this saga, but too much about the adult lives is unrevealed to make them entirely real. They, instead, become partially drawn "reasons" for what has happened in Carly's life. There will be some interest in this title because of its historical flavor. Children will relate to Carly's feelings, especially during the action when her dog is bitten by a coyote and may have contracted rabies.

AUNT NINA AND HER NEPHEWS AND NIECES by Franz Brandenberg. Illus. by Aliki. New York: Greenwillow, 1983. Younger

Aunt Nina's cat provides a gift for each niece and nephew, a kitten. Also AUNT NINA'S VISIT.

BACK YARD ANGEL by Judy Delton. Illus. by Leslie Morrill.
New York: Houghton Mifflin, 1983. Younger

Many young girls will relate to the feelings of Angel Oleary,
who has the responsibility of caring for her little brother, called
Rags.

BLATHERSKITE by Marian Potter. New York: William Morrow,
1980. Middle-Older

A portrayal of life during the depression years is set in a rural
Missouri town. Through the story of ten-year-old Maureen
McCracken, a spunky heroine, the reader learns about the economic problems of the times. The rural view of poverty includes
outdoor privies, hoboes, and work provided through the W.P.A.

BORROWED CHILDREN by George Ellen Lyon. New York:
Franklin Watts (Orchard Books), 1988. Middle-Older

When mama nearly dies during childbirth, Amanda is forced to
quit school and take care of the baby and the rest of the family.
Mandy develops nurturing instincts toward the baby, but regrets
being away from school and assuming adult responsibility.

After her mother improves, as a reward for her hard work,
Mandy is invited to spend Christmas in Memphis with her grandparents. Having always dreamed of the city and envisioned it as a
place of glamour and rich living, Mandy controls her protective
feelings about the baby and goes to Memphis. The story weakens at
this point when the author attempts to show that beneath the
glamour of the city, there is unhappiness. Mandy observes this as
she encounters her relatives in the city. The characterizations of the
city-dwellers are so slight that this portion becomes more message
than fiction.

THE BOY WHO WANTED A FAMILY by Shirley Gordon.
Pictures by Charles Robinson. New York: Harper and Row,
1980. Middle

This simple, warm story will help young people understand the
plight of older children needing and wanting adoption. After a brief
view of life in foster homes, the social worker tells Michael that he
is going to live with a woman who wishes to adopt him. It is hard for
Michael to believe that the adoption will materialize because one

adoption attempt has failed. He suffers through the months of waiting while enjoying his new mom and his new home. Finally the trip to court and the judge's approval occurs and Michael finally has a family. Few adoption stories actually deal with procedures of adoption. This is a one-parent adoption presented rather matter-of-factly.

CADY by Lillian Eige. Illus. by Jane Wentworth. New York: Harper and Row, 1987. Middle-Older

Cady, who has lived with several relatives over the years, finds himself in the care of Thea McVey. The early passages of the narrative cover his developing relationship with Thea, his newest foster parent. Having had many tenuous family relationships, Cady finds it hard to trust anyone. A bond grows between the two and Cady gradually accepts Thea as his friend. He begins to enjoy his life playing with the children from a neighboring family and watching the silent man who lives in a cabin on Thea's property.

The reader becomes involved at first in the painstaking day-to-day development of the relationship betweeen Cady and Thea; at another level is the mystery of the man in the cabin. Cady eventually discovers that the man is his father.

This mutilayered novel is concerned with identity, family, and relationships. Moreover it is a good environmental piece in that the mystery man (Cady's father) loves the foxes found in the nearby woods. Cady has observed him saving the foxes from being trapped. In the end, it is through their mutual love of the animals that Cady and his father begin to communicate. The reasons for the slow reconciliation between father and son are not quite clear, except that father is a recluse and has somehow separated himself from the norms of living. An explanation is given, but significant is the fact that changes have occurred which provide Cady with prospects for security.

CARROTS AND MIGGLE by Ardath Mayhar. New York: Atheneum, 1986. Middle-Older

Carrots faces the coming of Emiglia, her cousin who was born in Hungary and reared in London. Carrots wonders how this newcomer, near her own age, will fit in at their east Texas ranch. Mother, Carrots, and her little sister cooperate in running the farm. An uncle and his wife also assist. Life on the ranch is not easy and requires the help of everyone.

Emiglia is dubbed "Miggle" by Carrots little sister. Miggle interacts with the family with a superior attitude. She openly shows her disdain for those who work with their hands. The story follows the family's subtle and not too subtle confrontations with Miggle's prejudices. Even so a bond slowly develops between Carrots and Miggle. When Miggle has a chance to move to California and live with well-to-do members of the family, she refuses the option for a life-style similar to the one she had in the past—but this child of privilege still faces serious learning and adjusting before becoming a ranch hand.

Endorsement of those who work with their hands and of the family as a team is evident here.

CASSIE BINEGAR by Patricia MacLachlan. New York; Harper and Row, 1982. Middle-Older

Cassie is a member of a very colorful family, presented in the author's pithy characterizations. Cassie wishes for a more traditional life-style, until a writer comes to stay. Through her companionship with and adoration of the writer, Cassie comes to terms with her life and begins to accept her family and her circumstance.

CAT-MAN'S DAUGHTER by Barbara Abercrombie. New York: Harper and Row, 1983. Middle-Older

Shared custody is a strain on children, but the problem is even worse when the parents live respectively on the West and East Coasts. Kate travels from coast to coast, spending time in Los Angeles with her father, a TV star and with her mother, who lives in New York.

CAVE UNDER THE CITY by Harry Mazer. New York: Thomas Y. Crowell, 1986. Middle-Older

CAVE UNDER THE CITY is both a story of family and one of survival during the depression. Hard times experienced by many during this period are revealed through the plight of one family in the city.

When the story begins, things have already begun to get bad, but the family is intact. Changes occur rapidly when Tolly's father leaves for Baltimore to seek work. Soon after he leaves, Tolly's mother becomes ill and is hospitalized. When he and his younger brother, "Bubber," seek shelter with their grandmother, they find that she is also ill. The author, thus, swiftly and skillfully provides the circumstance in which the two young boys must survive alone. Their situation becomes most acute when they vacate the apartment to escape the authorities who would place them in a shelter.

The rest of the story traces the boys surviving in a city facing crisis. The two, at first, try to attend school, but are soon immersed in seeking shelter, finding food, escaping social workers, and learning to love and trust each other. The author presents scenes of the brothers stealing bread and milk, wearing dirty smelly clothes and shoes with holes, and begging for pennies to buy food. A vivid sense of the city is provided in the background. To all of this, tension and suspense is added because the children must return to the old apartment from time to time to check for news of their parents. On each of these occasions, there is the possibility of being caught by social workers.

The conclusion is a bit pat, but possible, when the children return to the apartment one day and find that their father is there. This resolution is made more real by the fact that the mother is still ill and will not return home immediately.

COME SING, JIMMY JO by Katherine Paterson. New York: Dutton (Lodestar Books), 1985. Older

Although this is story about growing up, a strong sense of family is present. The story discloses James's rise to popularity as a country-western singing star and in the background are his fears of public appearances and his family's secrets unfolding. It is the appearance of his biological father, whom Jimmy Jo has never known, which causes the serious conflicts. In the end, James, known publicly as Jimmy Jo Johnson, realizes that he doesn't have to accept the stranger as his father. The man he has known all of his life and who has supported him and been a part of his closely knit family is his real father.

The characterizations are good and the author evokes a sense of celebration with this family which loves to sing. Humor is interjected and a good picture of life in Appalachia is provided.

COUNTRY OF BROKEN STONE by Nancy Bond. New York: Atheneum, 1980. Older-Oldest

Modern family mores are portrayed when Penelope, her older brother, and her father follow her stepmother and her three younger children to the fells in northern England. Here, the new mother will participate in an archaeological dig. The historical mysteries surrounding the site of their residence and the dig, plus the normal anxieties of two families merging after marriage, provides interesting reading.

THE DANCING MADNESS by Mildred Ames. New York: Delacorte, 1980. Older

For older readers, a stark picture of the depression years is seen in this story narrated by twelve-year-old Mary Reilly. The title is chosen because Mary's older sister, jobless and depressed, decides to try winning money by participating in a dance marathon, popular at that time. Luckless in love, and unable to deal with the family's plight, the older girl drowns herself. Countering the pathetic picture of her sister, is an admirable characterization of Mary.

DANIEL'S DOG by Jo Allen Bogart. Illus. by Janet Wilson. New York: Scholastic (North Winds), 1990. Younger

Daniel, like many children, feels neglected because his mother spends so much time with his new sister. Of what use is she anyway? She can't play or throw a ball. Daniel invents a companion ghost dog, sent by his grandfather from heaven. When Daniel, later, realizes that his mother still loves him, the ghost dog is needed less often.

DAPHNE by Marilyn Kaye. New York: Harcourt Brace Jovanovich, 1987. Middle-Older

Daphne faces the conflicts of her first year at junior high school. She and her good friend, Annie, plan to face the changes together, until Daphne's older sisters intervene. The sisters, Cassie and Phoebe, offer advice about what Daphne should wear and what clubs she should join. Daphne finds herself signing up for unwanted extra-curricular activities. Jerry, a new friend at school, helps Daphne to confront her sisters and to join the creative writing class which she desires.

This is one of the better of the "Sister Series," which are all rather episodic. Young people having a hard time developing their own identity within the family or at school could identify with the main character. Pointed out is the fact that people are different, even in the same family. Valid issues are presented and unlike some stories, parents involve themselves in resolving their child's problem.

THE DAY WE MET by Pheobe Koehler. Illus. by the author. New York: Bradbury, 1990. Youngest

Adoptive parents tell about the anticipation of bringing their child home. The simple story places the adoption of a child on par with the birth of a child. Crayon illustrations show the preparations being made.

DEAR LOLA, OR HOW TO BUILD YOUR OWN FAMILY by Judie Angell. New York: Bradbury, 1980. Middle

Although many of the elements of survival seem unlikely in this story, it is entertaining reading and presents an unlikely family situation. Six children escape from the St. Theresa Home and make their way to the fruit groves in California. They settle in the town of Sweet River where they struggle to keep the "family" together.

THE DIVORCE EXPRESS by Paula Danziger. New York: Delacorte, 1982. Older

Fourteen-year-old Phoebe spends weekdays with her father in Woodstock, New York. On weekends, she commutes to New York to visit with her mother. Each weekend, the bus Phoebe rides carries so many children from divorced families that this trip to the city is called "The Divorce Express."

Phoebe becomes friendly with one of her fellow travelers. The story follows their evolving friendship but most importantly offers views of the way each family handles the divisions in their lives.

DIXIE STORMS by Barbara Hall. New York: Harcourt Brace Jovanovich, 1990. Older-Oldest

Fourteen-year-old Dutch is confronted with feelings of inadequacy when her sophisticated cousin, Norma, arrives at the family farm. Feeling somewhat like a country bumpkin in contrast to Norma with her city ways, Dutch sulks and rejects her cousin. Dutch fills her mind with dreams and hopes that her brother will reconcile with his estranged wife, Becky. After trying to manipulate a reconciliation, Dutch realizes that there will be no change. The author painstakingly pictures a character in the throes of adolescent anguish, learning about the complications which arise in family life. Simultaneously, the relationship between Dutch and her cousin develops from one of envy and suspicion to one of trust.

THE DOWNTOWN DAY by Linda Strauss. Illus. by the author. New York: Pantheon, 1983. Youngest-Younger

Views of extended families are growing more uncommon in children's fiction. In this simple story for younger readers, aunts enter the picture when Linda goes shopping with two aunts. Tension develops when her aunts' choices do not coincide with her own.

THE DREAM KEEPER by Margery Evernden. New York: Lothrop, Lee and Shepard, 1983. Middle-Older

At grandmother "Bobe's" house, father is a businessman, mother is a musician, and now young Becka shows musical talent. When the ailing grandmother, Bobe, decides to be moved to a rest home, Becka is very depressed. Later, Becka discovers tapes made by her beloved Bobe from which she learns more than she has ever known about her family history and especially Bobe's life. She learns of her grandmother's sacrifices in an odyssey of Jewish immigration from Russia.

GONE FISHING by Earlene Long. Illus. by Richard Brown. New York: Houghton Mifflin, 1984. Younger

What more traditional event could be found to show the love between father and son than in a picture story about father and son on a fishing trip together?

GRANDMAMA'S JOY by Eloise Greenfield. Illus. by Carole Byard. New York: Putnam, 1980. Younger

In another one of her positive presentations of Black families, the author tells the story of Rhondy who is raised by her grandmother.

THE GRANNY PROJECT by Anne Fine. New York: Farrar, Straus and Giroux, 1983. Middle

With some humor, a serious family problem is confronted as four children try to keep grandmother from being sent to a nursing home. Set in England.

HANNAH'S FANCY NOTIONS by Pat Ross. Illus. by Bert Dodson. New York: Viking, 1988. Middle

A story which portrays children fulfilling adult duties is this one set at the turn of the century. Hannah assumes responsibility for the household including her three younger sisters and her grieving father, after her mother dies. Her creative gift for her sister, made from wallpaper becomes the source for a family business and for her father's awakening from his doldrums.

HAPPILY EVER AFTER . . . ALMOST by Judie Wolkoff. Scarsdale, N.Y.: Bradbury Press, 1982. Middle

In the frontmatter pages of the book, a drawing of a family tree introduces the complexity of the familial relationships resulting when divorced parents remarry. There are two sets of grandparents on both sides and two sets of everyone else. There are two estranged parents lurking at the edges of this new family relationship. All of these complications are dealt with with hilarity and truth in this book. Amid the funny scenes, the reader encounters the problems faced in responding to the mother and father who exist outside of the marriage, and to the grandparents who are related and unrelated. The humor does not obscure the adult power plays which affect the progress of family life, shown through situational examples, during family gatherings, and during family emergencies.

HOMESICK: MY OWN STORY by Jean Fritz. Illus. by Margot Tomes. Putnam, 1982. Middle-Older

Some libraries may have this book in the biographical section, but many consider it fiction. The well-known author of children's books grew up in China where she attended a British school. She tells the the story of the year when she was ten years old. The brewing revolution in China and the unpopularity of foreigners are elements in the background, but central to the story are a young girl's feelings about herself and her family. Details about Chinese culture are seen through her eyes, with some slight condescension as Ms. Fritz includes incidents of her own childhood antics and of friendships formed. The most poignant portion of the story covers the family's expectancy of a child, and the subsequent birth and death of Jean's sister.

When it is no longer safe to be an American in China, the family returns to America. The book ends with historical notes and includes photographs of the family and the Chinese nanny.

THE HOUSE ON WALENSKA STREET by Charlotte Herman.

Illustrated by Susan Avishai. New York: Dutton, 1990. Middle

This is a very slight but warmly presented story for younger readers which offers a view of a Russian family in the early twentieth century. Simultaneously, the family is compared with an American counterpart through the exchange of letters. Leah reads about and dreams of immigrating to America, but the scenes of her family and their relationships to each other are warm and humorous. The repressive atmosphere in Russia is documented only slightly when soldiers come to search the house.

HOW I PUT MY MOTHER THROUGH COLLEGE by Corinne Gerson. New York: Atheneum, 1981. Middle-Older

Roles are partially reversed when Jessica's mother decides to return to college. Jessica encourages her mother, helps her find appropriate clothing to wear, and helps keep the household affairs moving along. Problems arise when mom starts dating a younger man and acting younger than her years. With humor and insight, all is resolved in the end.

I HAVE TWO FAMILIES by Doris Wild Helmering. Illus. by Heidi Palmer. New York: Abingdon, 1981. Younger.

Thoughts about her parents divorce are expressed by a young girl. This book will help younger children deal with some of their feelings about parents separating.

I, REBEKAH, TAKE YOU, THE LAWRENCES by Julia First. New York: Watts, 1981. Middle

Rebekah's story challenges some of the romanticized versions of adoption which appear in many books. When adopted by the Lawrences, this young girl experiences many problems.

I WILL CALL IT GEORGIE'S BLUES by Suzanne Newton. New York: Viking, 1983. Older-Oldest

This is a story portraying a dysfunctional family in which the father is a Baptist minister. He uses his position as father and minister to exert a sinister hold on his family. The horrors of mental abuse are readily evident in this gripping, thought-provoking novel.

I WISH DADDY DIDN'T DRINK SO MUCH by Judith Vigna.
   Illus. by the author. Whitman (Concept Books), 1988. Youngest.

   As in several of the books for older readers, this book reveals
the two faces of an alchoholic parent. The changes in personality are
reflected in this story for very young readers at Christmas, when
Lisa is upset by her father's drinking. Mrs. Field, a recovering
alchoholic offers information and comfort. This is not a book for
story hour programs, but could be used in parenting classes and
teenage discussions as mentioned in the programming section
below. A selection of such books could be offered to local mental
health and alchoholism prevention programs which often provide
counseling sessions for families which are disfunctional as a result of
alchoholism.

IF PHYLLIS WERE HERE by Gail Jarrow. Boston: Houghton
   Mifflin, 1987. Middle

   Family adjustment to change is the focus of this story which
shows Grandmother, Phyllis, suddenly becoming rich from winning
the lottery. With her new riches, Phyllis plans to move to Florida
leaving the household where she has played a major part.
   After Phyllis's departure, young Libby faces an empty house
when she returns from school and her parent's ineptness at handling
responsibilities which Phyllis had assumed. Later, when a housekeeper is hired, this intruder in Libby's life is not welcome,
especially when she nearly discards Libby's comic book collection.
   To this situation, the author adds social conflicts at school,
where Libby has become the target of Candace. Set upon ruining
Libby's reputation, Candace is even willing to let Libby be blamed
for stealing. With simple straightforward writing and a humorous
approach, the family's gradual adjustment and Libby's conquering
of the situation with Candace are dealt with.

IF YOU LISTEN by Charlotte Zolotow. Illus. by Marc Simont.
   New York: HarperCollins, 1980. Younger

   Feelings of the young are expressed through a small girl's
questions about whether her absentee father still loves her.

IN OUR HOUSE SCOTT IS MY BROTHER by Carole S. Adler.
   New York: Macmillan, 1980. Older

Divorce again is at issue in this story told by a thirteen-year-old boy. Some insight is shown to the adult side of the family's problems. Excellent for parenting collections.

IS ANYBODY THERE? by Eve Bunting. New York: Lippincott, 1988. Middle-Older

Marcus Miller is a thirteen-year-old "latchkey child." Although his mom is not at home when he arrives from school, Marcus has felt secure. The old lady who lives next door watches out for him and a lodger, Nick, lives upstairs in the house.

Never-the-less, it is frightening when things in the house begin to disappear. Marcus finds evidence that someone is entering his house while he and his mom are away. He is suspicious of Nick who, lately, has become close to his mom. His resentment of their relationship shows when he targets Nick as the culprit.

In the conclusion, the intruder is revealed as Nick's son, who has lived with his own mom since his parent's divorce. The story's concentration is on the mystery of the intruder, rather than on the issue of children being left alone. The problem of Nick's son has to be resolved along with the growing relationship between Nick and Marcus's mother. Emphasis in the closing passages is placed on resolving family problems.

THE ISLAND OF GHOSTS by Eilis Dillon. New York: Charles Scribner's, 1989. Older

Amid colorful scenes of life, family, community, and culture on a remote Irish Island, a mysterious story of two boys and their abduction by a reclusive American engineer is presented.

The two boys, Dara and Brendan have been coached by an engineer, George Webb, for the exams which would allow them to earn scholarships and to attend school on the mainland of Galway. Webb, devises a plan to keep the boys at home, being concerned that all the young people are leaving this place with which he is so fascinated. Webb abducts the boys through subterfuge, taking them to the Island of Ghosts. This nearby Island is surrounded by legends of its lost residents. The community views the Island of Ghosts with superstition and fear. Fears are overcome when a trip to the Island is required to rescue the two young boys from the clutches of their captor.

The story is well told and, with the elements of mystery, provides an entertaining introduction to family life in a different culture.

IT MUST HAVE BEEN THE FISH STICKS by Betty Bates. New York: Holiday House, 1982. Middle

New developments in family relationships are certain, after Brian finds out that his mother is really his stepmother. The resulting story documents Brian's confusion and hurt, and discovery of his past.

JESSE AND ABE by Rachel Isadora. Illus. by the author, New York: Greenwillow, 1981. Younger

This picture story reveals Jesse's realization that his grandfather is an important part of his life.

JUST AN OVERNIGHT GUEST by Eleanora E. Tate. New York: Dial, 1980. Middle

A young ten year old tells the story of the time in her life when she has to confront the intrusion into her life and family by an "overnight guest."

It's terrible to be ten years old and have a special relationship with your mother, father and sister, and suddenly to be confronted by a four-year-old daughter of "white trash." Even more painful is the fact that the four year old is allowed to get away with things you would not have been allowed to do. She is allowed to sleep in your bed and is not scolded for being a bed wetter, and for breaking your special collection of shells.

Ten-year-old Margie's story is set in rural North Carolina amid small town gossip, and separate communities of Black and White. Everyone knows that the young child, Ethel, is "half white" and her presence with the family prompts negative reactions. Margie resents having the child around, and hates having her wear her favorite old dresses even if they are too small . . . but nothing is worse than having the intruder capture her father's attention and then to find that outsider will become a permanent addition to the family.

The reader learns that Ethel is a relative, the child of Uncle Jake, mother's brother. The family conflicts are lovingly resolved and adjustment to the family addition seems probable.

JUST LIKE A REAL FAMILY by Kristi D. Holl. New York:
Atheneum, 1983. Middle-Older

In many cities around the country young people are being
paired with seniors for their mutual gratification. This story
documents that process. June Finch is twelve when her class starts
a project to adopt grandmothers from a retirement home.

KAREN'S SISTER by Elizabeth McHugh. New York: Greenwillow, 1983. Middle

An unusual adoptive family story follows the activities of
Karen, who is a Korean adoptee; her mother who does not plan to
marry; her grandmother who is zany and loving; and Tae Ja who is
the new addition to the family.
There are many humorous and poignant incidents which bring
the family together in their own special way as Tae Ja is integrated
into the family.
Beneath the surface is grandmother's constant wish that her
daughter should marry. Although mom has strenuously objected to
marraige, she meets John and suddenly announces her intent to
wed.
Such a warm and humorous story might make all children wish
to be adopted. What other family has so much fun? In fact, the story
seems a bit unrealistic and mom's sudden reversal to being the
marrying kind seems a cop-out. The book is, however, fun to read.

LET THE CIRCLE BE UNBROKEN by Mildred Taylor. New
York: Dial, 1981. Older

The novel follows the lives of the same family presented by the
author in ROLL OF THUNDER HEAR MY CRY, in which that
family's strength and resiliency in the face of racial prejudice are
documented. This story further looks at family unity while divulg-
ing critical aspects of relationships between Blacks and Whites in a
Southern setting.

LYDIA by Marilyn Kaye. New York: Harcourt Brace Jovanovich,
1987 (Sister Series). Middle-Older

At fourteen, Lydia is the oldest of the Gray sisters. She is a
spirited nonconformist. Her father, editor of the local newspaper,
gives her the idea for starting an alternative paper at the Cedar Park

Junior High School. After an editorial board is formed, the paper's first line of attack is on the food in the cafeteria. The success of this campaign inflates Lydia's ego, which quickly deflates when her next campaign to allow girls on the football team is not successful. While learning something about making assumptions and being rejected, Lydia receives surprising support from the co-captains of the football team.

Books in the "Sister Series" are designed as episodic glances at the divergent personalities of and the conflicts between sisters.

MAMA ONE, MAMA TWO by Patricia MacLachlan. Illus. by Ruth Lercher Bornstein. New York: HarperCollins, 1982. Younger

Reinforcing the fact that there are times when foster parents are necessary and presenting a positive picture of that process, this story presents a foster family situation while the mother is away in therapy.

THE MOST BEAUTIFUL PLACE IN THE WORLD by Ann Cameron. Illus. by Thomas B. Allen. New York: Alfred A. Knopf, 1988. Younger

Juan describes his home in Guatemala. The village in which he lives is pictured as being very beautiful, although obviously an area of great poverty. Juan's mother is about to remarry and her prospective husband does not want a ready-made family. Juan goes to live with his grandmother who puts him to work as a shoeshine boy. The young child learns to read street signs by asking others the names. He would like more than anything to go to school and learn to read. Because Juan has assumed work responsibility at such an early age, he has become wise beyond his years. Grandmother admits that she had forgotten that her grandchild is only seven years old. She allows Juan to attend school and in a conversation between the two about the most beautiful place in the world, Grandmother says it is "Any place you can hold your head up," and Juan says it is "Where you love somebody and you know that person loves you."

The rejection of Juan by his mother is not dealt with in any depth in this simple book. How could grandmother not have some sense of his tender years? These are the questions for which many children will want answers. The sentimentality does not mask these omissions.

MY DAD IS REALLY SOMETHING by Lois Osborn. Illus. by the author. New York: Whitman, 1983. Younger

Harry appreciates his own dad, when he learns that his friend's dad is not what he is supposed to be.

MY SISTER'S KEEPER by Beverly Butler. New York: Dodd, Mead, 1980. Older-Oldest

The plot is set during the drought years of 1971, when Mary James has been sent to live with her sister Clara who is having another child. Mary develops a crush on her sister's husband, Ellery. She is harboring guilt about her feelings when the fires come. The whole community has to flee for their lives as fire races through the dry woods.

There are vivid scenes of family members being separated from each other in the resulting turmoil. In the confusion, Mary loses her nephew, Tat.

After the fire, the process of rebuilding is clouded by the fact that Tat has not been found. Trauma and sorrow have made Mary a more mature person. She begins to view Ellery's weaknesses and is drawn to a strong and resilient man who helps her search for Tat. In the end, Tat is found and the family goes on to rebuild. Meanwhile Mary has grown up through her close encounter with disaster.

MY WAR WITH GOGGLE-EYES by Anne Fine. Boston, Toronto, London: Little, Brown and Company (Joy Street Books), 1989. Middle-Older

This story about divorced parents finding new partners and the effect of that on young people is structured differently from most. When a classmate of Kitty's arrives at school distraught and in tears, Kitty is selected by her teacher to leave class and comfort the tearful girl. Kitty's selection is not by accident, the teacher is aware that Kitty has experienced the problem her classmate is facing—adjustment to her mother's new mate. The teacher has learned the details of Kitty's experience because she has told her story in writings for class.

In the isolation of a cloakroom, Kitty reveals the entire story for her classmate's benefit. Told in first person, the narrative documents Kitty's feelings of alienation when her own mother chose a new partner, "Goggle-Eyes." In the cloakroom, hidden away from everyone, details of her gradual adjustment to the new relationship are disclosed.

The structure works well and Kitty's story is told with grandeur and humor. Additional humor is interjected with breaks in the

narrative when friends, classmates, and the teacher come periodi-
cally to the cloakroom door, to monitor the situation within. Kitty's
story proves helpful to her classmate.

This title should also be noted for its views on politics and the
environment. As Kitty's story evolves we find that she and her
mother are regular demonstrators at various enviromental and
nuclear protests. This is one of the bones of contention between
Kitty, and Goggle-Eyes—that he does not participate in nor
understand the commitment of the demonstrators. There are
healthy passages on protest methodology and on which selected
political actions bring the best results.

NELDA by Pat Edwards. Boston: Houghton Mifflin, 1987. Middle-
Older

Nelda Shanks lives with the rest of her family of migrant
workers in a tent near the fields. She often dreams of being rich,
and Elberta, a self proclaimed fortune teller convinces Nelda that
her dreams will come true.

The family is discovered by Miss Mattie May, a well-to-
do woman who becomes the family's benefactor. In exchange
for her kindnesses, Miss Mattie wants one of the children to
come and live with her. Nelda conspires so that she will be
chosen to live with Miss Mattie, but she soon finds that life
apart from her family is very lonely. In spite of having new
clothes and a room of her own, Nelda misses the warmth of her
family. She becomes especially upset when she learns that the
family plans to move on, following the crops. Not wanting to
be left behind, and being a born conniver, Nelda finds a way to
extricate herself from the situation. Her sister, who is enamored
with a local boy and wishes to stay, remains with the lonely old
woman.

Nelda's capers have not quite ended for there is one more
problem to solve. With a new baby in the family, Nelda realizes that
it is time for the family to find a real home. Her grandmother,
alienated from her daughter for marrying a n'er-do-well, has a place
big enough to accommodate them. As usual, Nelda cleverly finds
the way.

This humorous mix of realism and fancifulness provides a
different (somewhat romanticized) picture of migrant life. Amid
the poverty and bleakness, the need for love, security and family is
emphasized. The story works only because this seems to be the
author's intent.

THE NIGHT SWIMMERS by Betsy Byars. Illus. by Troy Howell.
New York: Delacorte, 1980. Middle

Retta, named after Loretta Lynn; Johnny, named after Johnny
Cash; and Roy named after Roy Acuff; are the "night swimmers."
Their father, Shorty, leaves the children alone at night while he
performs, hoping to be a country-western singing star.

Since their mother died, Retta has been in charge of her
two brothers. She manages fairly well until the night that Roy
nearly drowns. The children have been sneaking out at night,
and swimming in the pool at a neighbor's house. The incident at
"the Colonel's" pool causes Shorty to reconsider his role and
responsibilities as a father. Change in the children's lives is
foreseen.

This story focuses on a modern family with young children
forced into self-supervision.

NO SCARLET RIBBONS by Susan Terris. New York: Farrar,
Straus and Giroux, 1981. Older

With an unusual protagonist, the author succeeds in exposing
problems resulting from the fusion of two families after parents
with older children remarry.

Rachel has looked forward to the marriage of her mother to
Norm, a junior high school teacher. She becomes disenchanted,
however, when her visions of blissful family life do not materialize.
She resents the time Norm and her Mother spend together, while
the family gatherings and outings Rachel attempts to arrange fail
miserably.

Rachel's attempts to sabotage the marriage are outrageous, but
are true to the characterization developed by the author. Taunting
her new stepbrother with sexual overtures and manipulated togetherness, she causes a fight between her parents. For once, in a
children's book, parents are allowed to have an argument, complete
with throwing books, and shouting. After the argument, Rachel
begins to mellow and change her ways.

ODD GIRL OUT by Joan Lingard. London: Elsevier/Nelson, 1978.
Older

Fourteen-year-old Ellen is nearly six feet tall, redheaded, and
difficult. When her mother decides to remarry, Ellen is hostile. She
feels that the marriage means a betrayal of her dead father. All of

these years, rather than discuss the situation, Ellen's mother has let her believe that her father was dead. While Ellen worshipped what she thought was his memory, the father has been alive and well. He has remarried and has a family in Australia.

Confrontation between Ellen and her mother occurs when mother remarries and Ellen is forced to move with the newly-weds to another part of town. Ellen misses her friends and refuses to accept overtures from her stepfather to make her more comfortable. Not until then does her mother decide to tell Ellen the truth.

A subplot to the mother-daughter relationship evolves as Ellen forms an attachment to Nicholas, a much older man, who teaches her piano. With the help of Nicholas, her young friends, and her mother's friend, Ellen faces the complex emotions confronting her. She begins a gradual adjustment.

Although set in England, the situations portraying individual adjustment and growth are universal. The emotional turmoil experienced by the main character rings true.

ONE THING FOR SURE by David Gifaldi. Boston: Houghton Mifflin (Clarion Books), 1986. Older-Oldest

Twelve-year-old Dylan refuses to visit his luckless father who is serving time in an Oregon jail for illegally cutting timber. During the summer, Dylan meets Amy, who is visiting from Chicago. The developing friendship helps Dylan to face emotions which he has repressed.

Inadvertently, Amy also provides Dylan with a way to outwit former friends who have ostracized Dylan since his father's incarceration. Amy and Dylan develop a unique idea for making money during the summer. Since Amy is a camera buff, they decide to use her talents and take pictures of her dog in various poses and costumes. From the pictures, they make postcards to sell. The camera is also used at the local swimming hole to take nude pictures of the boys who have been taunting Dylan. The threat to expose these pictures gives Dylan leverage over them.

Family, friendship, peer pressures are all ingredients of the story. Winning acceptance on one's own terms is also emphasized. Dylan finally gains enough self confidence to visit his father and to confront his parents about his feelings.

OUT OF LOVE by Hilma Wolitzer. New York: Farrar, Straus and Giroux, 1976. Middle-Older

Teddy has not accepted her parents' divorce. It is hard for her to believe that her father could have written love letters (which she has secretly read) to her mother and not still love her. On occasion, Teddy slips into her mother's closet and reads the letters which help keep her hopes alive that her parents will reconcile. These hopes lie in the face of the fact that her father has remarried.

Comparing her mother to her father's new wife, Teddy views her mother as dowdy in contrast to her father's younger, slimmer, and more beautiful new companion. With this scenario, the author takes the reader through the painful process of realization that the change in Teddy's life is permanent.

The author relieves the reader from pathos by showing other elements of Kathy's life: situations at school, discussions with her friend Maya Goldstein (who has her own gripes about family life), and the development of her first relationship with a boy. Kathy's campaign to change her mother and to have her win her husband back is shockingly ended when her father announces that his new wife is pregnant. For the first time, mother commiserates with Kathy about her feelings. They talk about love lost and the old letters are thrown away. Kathy's agonies are softened by her own realizations (aided by talks with her aunt) that beauty is in the eye of the beholder. She also involves herself in the resolution of Maya's trials with her overprotective family. The pain of adjustment to divorce is made evident in this novel and the author presents a character who grows and learns to look ahead. Adult characters are much more than mere backdrops.

PIP AND EMMA by Katherine Jay Bacon. New York: Atheneum, 1986. Older

A story reflecting the new independence shown by mothers in today's world presents Pip and Emma spending the summer in Vermont with their grandmother, while their mother goes off to Europe to study painting. Adventures reflect the complexities of modern family life.

RACHEL CHANCE by Jean Thesman. Houghton Mifflin, Boston, 1990. Older

Fifteen-year-old Rachel doesn't care that people call her baby brother Ryder "illegitimate." She loves him, and secretly holds information about Ryder's father. She is happy that her mother rejects the insistence of the minister that the child should be given up for adoption. Then, one day, Ryder disappears, and the whole family mourns his loss.

Rachel decides that something must be done, someone has to find the baby or they may never see him again. The rest of the story follows Rachel's eventually successful attempts to find and rescue Ryder. The story presents a strong sense of family and a strong young female character, vulnerable but able to make her own decisions.

REASONS TO STAY by Margaret Froehlich. New York: Houghton Mifflin, 1986. Older

Babe, the middle child, holds her makeshift family together after her mother dies. There is much that Babe does not understand about her undependable father and her mother's past relationships. She is aware of the differences between herself, her older sister Florence, and brother, Rivius. Although nagging questions haunt her, Babe loves her sister and her baby brother. As much as she would like to know more about her past, she concentrates on keeping the family together.

Fate takes the family close to the area where Babe's mother formerly lived. After a motoring accident, the children are taken in by the Shaw family. For the first time, the children experience a secure and nourishing lifestyle. Babe, however, still wishes to find answers about herself and leaves temporarily seeking what she believes is her real family.

What Babe learns is not pleasant, but she at least understands more about her mother's past and about her own parentage. Rain and floods come, symbolizing the washing away of the old life. The new life begins when the father is drowned and the Shaws adopt the three children.

Some aspects of Babe's quest do not seem entirely credible. This distracts only slightly from what altogether is an adequate chronicle of a farm family in distress.

SAY CHEESE by Betty Bates. Drawings by Jim Spence. New York: Holiday House, 1984. Middle

Because she has heard her father singing old songs around the house, Christy Hooper is able to "name that song" on a radio contest. After winning one hundred dollars, should she be selfish and buy herself a dress or buy something for the whole family? Important for its presentation of a large loving family—mother, father, two sisters and two brothers, the story presents a message about sharing.

SECOND STAR TO THE RIGHT by Deborah Hautzig. New York: Greenwillow, 1981. Older

Presented are family relationships which may contribute to or exacerbate the condition of anorexia nervosa, a growing problem among teenage girls. Chronicled are aspects of the problem and its correction.

SEND NO BLESSINGS by Phyllis Reynolds Naylor. New York: Atheneum, 1990. Older

One thing missing from today's fiction which was portrayed in the past is the large, boisterous, happy family. Large families more often than not find themselves in a situation of poverty as is true of this story. Fifteen-year-old Beth Herndon is the oldest child, with seven siblings. She assumes a large part of the responsibility for care of the younger children. Her prayer is that God will "send no more blessings," meaning that her mother will have no more children.

The family lives in the tight quarters of a trailer in the hill country of West Virginia. Life is hard for many in this area.

Beth strikes up a relationship with a local beau but decides that if she marries him, her life will be no better than her mothers. With the help of her teachers, Beth aims for a better life.

SOMEONE'S MOTHER IS MISSING by Harry Mazer. Delacorte, 1990. Older

Although the style of using alternating main characters presenting their viewpoints has been used by several authors, Mazer has the ability to present in depth characterizations within this device. Liza's father dies and the family's illusory wealth has disappeared. They face poverty for the first time. Lisa's mother is incapable of handling the situation and walks out leaving Lisa and her little sister, Robin, to cope alone.

Lisa seeks shelter with her cousins who, formerly, have been considered beneath Lisa's family in sophistication and wealth. The rest of the story, told alternately from Lisa's and Sam's point of view, exposes attitudes about economic class, similar to CARROTS AND MIGGLE. When the two cousins combine forces to find Lisa's mother, their understandings of what life is about are ameliorated and they grow closer. Many children will not be able to empathize with Lisa's loss of status, but the author presents an understandable character. Sam presents the point of view from which many will relate to the story.

STAR SHINE by Constance Greene. New York: Viking, 1985. Middle-Older

Jenny and her sister Mary learn to take care of themselves, when their stage struck mother leaves home to join a summer theatre group. The girls worry about their dad and speculate about his turning to another woman.

When a movie company comes to town seeking extras among the townspeople, Jenny lands a part. Through her participation in movie making. Jenny learns a lot about herself, gains confidence and makes friends with Scott, the heartthrob of the junior crowd.

Slight and humorous, the story is built on the background of family relationships and tensions. Some sibling jealousies are exposed when Mary is rejected and Jenny gets a part in the movie. Finally, the mother returns home. Disappointed in her stage adventures, she becomes involved in her daughter's success.

STORY FOR A BLACK NIGHT by Bess Clayton. New York: Houghton Mifflin, 1982. Older

The rhythms and nuances of this story told by a Liberian father to his own children, presents a warm picture of family in a different culture, although the father's story is a sad one.

STREETS OF GOLD by Karen Branson. New York: Putnam, 1981. Older-Oldest

The author of POTATO EATERS, about the Irish famine of 1846, gives us an immigrant story about an Irish family. Beginning with grim scenes on the ship, the story follows the family to New York where views of poverty, the slums and cultural prejudice are seen. At first, the interjection of the Underground Railroad and scenes showing assistance given to escaping slaves seemed obtrusive, but later the same system is used to manage the father's escape when he finds himself in trouble.

Fourteen-year-old Maureen O'Conner, her father and two brothers arrive in New York and find shelter in a rooming house. Sharing one room, they begin their life of "promise." While

Maureen assumes the role of mother, the boys attend school. One brother becomes an excellent student and later receives a scholarship, while the other becomes involved in Irish gangs, reacting violently to the prejudices and rejection often encountered. Father goes off to seek work in the mines. It is during this period that he gets himself in trouble with the owners.

Meanwhile, Maureen accidently meets a young Englishman who befriended her on the boat trip. They fall in love and make plans to move to Saint Louis where they expect to improve their plight.

The language is colorful, and some of the scenes are poignant; however, the author presents many threads that are not dealt with in as much depth as possible. Prejudice is talked about, but not felt. The reasons for the father's need to escape are not altogether clear. Even so, readers can gain insight to this period from this novel. The critical effects of poverty and need upon a family are very apparent.

THAT'S ONE ORNERY ORPHAN by Patricia Beatty. William Morrow and Co, 1980. Middle-Older

Readers get an introduction to adoption practices of the past but most of all they follow the adventures of an older, feisty, female orphan called Hallie.

After arriving at an orphanage, Hallie finds that many people are not seeking older orphans to give them a home but to make workers of them. She especially doesn't want to be selected by the German "sodbuster," Otto. After several colorful and sometimes humorous misadventures, being placed in homes and subsequently returned to the orphanage, placement at Otto's becomes a reality. Hallie experiences her most pleasant surprise when she realizes that Otto and his wife really want a daughter, someone to be a member of the family.

THINGS WON'T BE THE SAME by Kathryn Ewing. New York: Harcourt Brace Jovanovich, 1980. Middle

When her divorced mother decides to remarry, Matty Benson is sure that "things won't be the same." She likes her mother's prospective husband well enough, but is faced with too many changes in her life. The worse is that she will have to spend the summer in San Francisco with her natural father, whom she hardly knows. Upon her return home, having thoroughly and surprisingly

enjoyed the visit with her father, Matty's anxieties surface again.
Now she faces adjustment to her stepfather and her stepsiblings.
Matty adjusts to her step-family over time.

TOUGH TIFFANY by Belinda Hurmence. New York: Doubleday, 1980. Middle-Older

A strong, young, Black female protagonist and views of family
life amid poverty in rural North Carolina are seen in the story. Told
against the background of real and varied characters is the story of
eleven-year-old Tiffany. Tiffany's father works steadily but does
not earn enough money to keep the bills paid, especially those bills
made by Tiffany's mother, a dreamer and spendthrift. Tiffany's
ingenuity helps to resolve the family's financial situation and to
resolve other problems.

The story is told with humor and an appealing flavor which
should make it interesting to readers from all cultures. Although
the focus is on Tiffany, the strengths gained from family and
community are evident. Tiffany gains insights from aunts, grandparents, and others in the community. It is especially rewarding to find
the father emerging with great strength of character. He is the one
who objects to the marraige of Tiffany's sister to the father of her
child, only for convenience and to save face.

WAIT TILL HELEN COMES, a ghost story by Mary Downing
Hahn. New York: Clarion, 1986. Middle-Older

Molly and Michael move into a converted church in the
country with their mother and her new husband, Dave. They miss
their old friends and they dislike Dave's weird daughter, Heather,
whose mother died in a mysterious fire.

Heather becomes obsessed with a small tombstone hidden
in the graveyard near the church. The tombstone bears her ini-
tials. Molly gradually becomes engrossed in saving her stepsister
from her obsession. Heather's strange behavior is based on the
need to release the sorrow and fear resulting from her mother's
death.

WHEN I AM OLD WITH YOU by Angela Johnson. Illus. by
David Soman. New York: Watts, 1990. Younger

A small Black child imagines the future when he will be as old
as his grandaddy. He supposes that they will go fishing and have

other fun together. The warmth and togetherness of the two is illustrated with beautiful watercolor paintings.

YOU PUT UP WITH ME, I'LL PUT UP WITH YOU by Barbara
  Corcoran. New York: Atheneum, 1987. Older

The grouping formed when Kelly's mother and two of her friends combine resources to open a restaurant in an old school house is more like a "cooperative" than a family. Kelly has been an only child and since her father's death she and her mother have always lived alone. Now, Kelly must share her room with Ester, daughter of one of the partners. Two younger children are also added to the household.

Kelly's alienation and conflict are exhibited in many ways culminating in a plan to sabotage the business operation, enlisting the help of her friend Rhonda, who lives next door. The conflicts and gradual adjustment are different from those of families brought together through marraige. The emphasis here is on learning to share while at the same time accepting individuality.

PROGRAMMING SUGGESTIONS FOR SECTION II

1. Assign parts, and read aloud one act plays which deal with issues of friendship and family. Schools and libraries might consider forming a formal drama group specifically designed to discuss and present plays, dramatic readings, poetry, etc. which deal with social issues. This group might even want to try some rap music. Source: CENTER STAGE: ONE ACT PLAYS FOR TEENAGE READERS AND ACTORS by Donald R. Gallo. HarperCollins, 1990 with plays which focus on teenage problems, some of which deal with family situations.

2. Many libraries have formed "parents with toddlers" programs. These programs could be especially productive if they were designed to train parents in reading aloud skills and in selecting materials. Propose places that attendees may share these skills and help spread the word to other parents. Head Start, WIC (Women, Infants, and Children) programs, and health centers are examples of places where librarians can meet low-income mothers and provide such training. This way the families who need the experience most can be reached.

3. Hold baby-sitting classes for teens. These can include reading materials about young children and families so that older children understand more about relating to the young. Through discussion of these materials, participants also gain parenting skills.

4. Prepare a bulletin board titled FAMILY. Under Grandparents, place covers and/or titles from a multicultural list of books portraying grandparents, under Fathers, books which focus on father, under Mother, books which have strong presentations of mothers. Add Aunts, Uncles, etc. Children could be asked to bring pictures for such a bulletin board. Each child will have at least one of these relatives for whom he or she can contribute a picture.

5. Using the book CRICKET AND THE CRACKERBOX KID, read aloud and hold the trial before telling listeners how the story ended.

6. Using the form of the "write your own story" books, ask the class or discussion group to provide the ending to a plot from a book. Compare with the author's resolution. Make up situations or take them from books on a reading list. Discuss the situation, then move to presentation of books with this situation or similar ones presented. This can be done by librarians before presenting a booktalk, or by teachers to provide motivation for reading.

7. Pen pal clubs could be formed between libraries or classes in different cultural or income level neighborhoods. Teachers and librarians should supervise this first name only—no address communication. After a period of time a party could be held with parents invited. Given an opportunity to write letters might help some children feel less isolated. Chances to talk about their "pals" should be allowed.

8. Play "THE FAMILY GAME" in which a situation from a book title is presented. Participants are assigned the roles of book characters, father, mother, the protagonist, a neighbor who is involved, etc. Using situations from novels, questions are asked of each. What would you do? What would you say? This game could be devised appropriately for younger to the oldest readers. A similar game could be devised to gain insights into friendship and peer presssures. This differs slightly from the

exercise of providing the ending or resolution to a story because several situations can be used from one book.

9. Invite representatives from organizations for the homeless to classrooms or libraries. Children can hold discussions with such leaders after reading titles dealing with the homeless.

10. For socialization, do mixer exercises with children who attend pre-school or other story-hour programs. After making notes of things as the children enter, the mixer exercise could be as simple as "Find the person wearing yellow socks" and "Tell me their name." Do this exercise until you have included all the children. Hold these sessions at the end of the story hour so as not to disrupt the program. If parents are present they could also participate.

11. Plan classroom exercises and activities in libraries in which children do things as groups. Make sure these groups are not self selected.

12. Libraries could try the exercise which has been documented in books and on television in which teens are given an egg or another object, which they must treat as a baby. They can't leave it alone, they must make sure it is kept warm, etc. (see FIRST THE EGG [page 41] by Louise Moeri.) Essays could be written about the process.

13. Provide a display from books, archives, etc., showing pictures, titled "THE AMERICAN FAMILY, A HISTORICAL PROGRESSION." Be sure to seek sources which will allow your display to reflect minority cultures along with others. Pictures could be borrowed from area families. Many will have portraits of family from different eras.

14. A list of books which families could read together could be printed on the back of a listing of local activities provided for families.

15. Invite foreign exchange students to speak about the differences in family life in their countries and what they have observed here. If they have pictures, turn them into a slide presentation.

16. Form a "Teens Talk" or "Soap Box" series in which teens are interviewed about matters of family. Pattern it after "The Soap Box" series, available on video from PBS.

SELECTED AUDIOVISUALS

Each group of books is a suggested few which could be used with the video or film. Others are available in the text and in references listed in SOURCES AND NOTES.

1. Family Life
TEEN FATHER, videocassette, color, 34 min. $250 (Older)
Use with:
Someone to Love Me by Eyerly
Hey Kid! Does She Love Me? by Mazer (Both of these books reviewed in section on SEXUALITY.) Mazer's books should always be considered in discussions of various issues of family life with adolescents.

2. Individual Differences—Families (Variety of Family Structure)
SONGS FOR US: APPRECIATING DIFFERENCES, Videocassette, color 9:45 min. With Teacher's Guide. $250 (Younger) Use with:
Amish Adventure by Smucker
Hannah's Alaska by Reiser
Hotel Boy by Kaufman
Jamaica's Find by Havill
Aunt Nina and Her Nephews and Nieces by Aliki
Gone Fishing by Long
Grandmama's Joy by Greenfield
Mama One, Mama Two by MacLachlan

3. Families—Problems—Alcoholism, Abuse, Etc.
COPING WITH TROUBLE AT HOME, Videocassette, 68 min. With Teacher's Guide, $159. Filmstrip, $159 (Middle)
Use with:
Borrowed Children by Lyon
Hannah's Fancy Notions by Dodson
I Have Two Families by Helmering
I Will Call It Georgie's Blues by Newton
If You Listen by Zolotow

4. Families—Problems—Relieving Childhood Guilt
FAMILIES IN TROUBLE: LEARNING TO COPE, Videocassette. 32 min. With Teacher's Guide. $205. (Older) Use with:
The Moonlight Man by Fox
No Scarlet Ribbons by Terris

Odd Girl Out by Lingard
Rachel Chance by Thesman
Second Star to the Right by Hautzig
Fly Free by Adler
The Reason to Stay by Froelich
The Village by the Sea by Fox

5. Families—Divorce—Effects on Children
   IMPACT OF DIVORCE ON THE FAMILY, Videocassette, 15
   min. With Teacher's Guide. $39. (Older) Use with:
   Out of Love by Wolitzer
   Cat Man's Daughter by Abercrombie
   The Divorce Express by Danzinger
   In Our House, Scott is My Brother by Adler
   Last One Home by Osborne
   Something to Count by Moore

6. Families—Single Parent
   IMPACTS OF SINGLE PARENTS, Videocassette. 14 min.
   With Teacher's Guide. $39. (Oldest) Use with:
   Same as 1.
   The Crazies and Sam by Morris
   Is Anybody There? by Bunting

7. Families (Helping Each Other—Songs and Pantomime)
   ME AND MY FAMILY, Videocassette, 12 min. With An
   Activity Book. $109.95. (Younger-Middle) Use with:
   Backyard Angel by Delton
   The Downtown Day by Strauss
   Jesse and Me by Isadora

8. School—Peers—Adolescence
   DEGRASSI HIGH (SERIES), 16 mm or Videocassette, 15
   Films, 30 min. ea. With Teacher's Guide. Films, $535 ea.,
   Video, $250 ea. (Older-Oldest)

9. Adolescence—Teen Pressures—Case Histories
   FIGHTING BACK: FACING TEENAGE DEPRESSION,
   Videocassette, 30 min. With Teacher's Guide. $205. (Older)
   Use with:
   The Fastest Friend in the West by Grove

10. Socialization
    IN TOBY WE TRUST. Videocassette, 15 min. With Teacher's

Guide. (Younger) Use with:
Alfie Gives a Hand by Hughes
The Birthday Party by Oxenbury (and others by this author)
Henry's Happy Birthday Party by Keller
I'm Calling Molly by Kurtz
The Missing Tooth by Cole

11. Socialization
A KIDS GUIDE TO GETTING ALONG WITH EACH
OTHER. Videocassette, 43 min., With Teacher's Guide,
Video, $119, Filmstrip, $119. (Middle) Use with:
Hating Alison Ashley by Klein
Love From a Fifth Grade Celebrity by Giff
Rachel Vellars, How Could You? by Fisher
Bathing Ugly by Busselle

12. Adolescence—Pressures
THE TOUGH DECISIONS: HOW TO MAKE THEM.
Videocassette, 31 min. With Teacher's Guide. $185. (Older)
Use with:
Janet Hamm Needs a Date for the Dance by Bunting
Is It Them? or Is It Me? by Haven
The Method by Walker
More Than Meets the Eye by Betancourt
Picking Up the Pieces by Bates

13. Friendship
THE VALUE OF BEING A FRIEND (THE VALUE SE-
RIES). 18 min., With Teacher's Guide. 16 mm., $425. Video.
$380. (Younger-Middle)
THE VALUE OF TEAMWORK,16 mm. or Video, 15 min.
16mm., $355, Video, $320. (Younger-Middle)
Big Base Hit and *Making the Team* by Hughes
Eating Crow by Hopkins

14. Peer Pressures
WHEN THE PRESSURE'S ON: GROUPS AND YOU.
Videocassette, 20 min., With Teacher's Guide. (Middle-Older)
Use with:
Friends First by McDonnell
Just Friends by Klein
The Trial of Anna Cotman by Alcock
Whose Side Are You On? by Moore

15. Families—Similarities and Differences
    FAMILIES ARE DIFFERENT AND ALIKE. 16 mm or video.
    12-15 min. 16 mm, $380, video, 250. (Younger) Use with:
    Same as 2.

16. Families—Migrant
    ANGEL AND BIG JOE. 16 mm, 27 min., color. Learning
    Corporation. (Middle-Older) Use with:
    Nelda by Pat Edwards

17. Families—adoptive—mixed—large
    WHO ARE THE DEBOLTS? 16mm, 72 min., color. Pyramid,
    All Ages. Use with:
    The Boy Who Wanted a Family by Gordon
    I Rebekah Take You the Lawrences by First
    Karen's Sister by McHugh
    That's One Ornery Orphan by Beatty

18. Families—Sibling
    PROMOTING WHOLESOME SIBLING RELATION-
    SHIPS. Videocassette, 12 min. With Teacher's Guide. Mid-
    west Productions. $39.00. (Older-Oldest) Use with:
    Daphne and others in the SISTERS SERIES by Kaye
    Get lost Little Brother by Adler
    Gowie Corby Plays Chicken by Kemp

19. Pairings and Groupings—Dating—Group Interaction
    BUILDING SELF CONFIDENCE. Videocassette, color, 390
    min. With Teachers Guide. $205. (Older-Oldest) Use with:
    The Method by Walker
    More Than Meets the Eye by Betancourt
    The Season of Good Wishes by Prochazkova

20. Friendship—Adolescence
    FRIENDSHIP; THE GOOD TIMES THE BAD TIMES.
    color, 30 min. With Teacher's Guide. $185 (Middle-Older)
    Use with:
    Between Friends by Garrigue
    Risk and Roses by Slepian
    The Runaways by Thomas
    Salted Lemons by Smith
    Thank You Dr. Martin Luther King Jr. by Tate
    They're All Named Wildfire by Springer
    Today Fifth Grade Tomorrow the World by Ransom

SECTION III
VIEWS OF THE WORLD

People and the Environment
Religion and Politics
War and Peace
Celebration of Life and Death

In his analysis of Piaget's findings, Elkind writes, "Too often we have a narrow view of learning and assume the child is learning only when he is acquiring what we want him to learn; a 'slowlearner' is one who does not acquire the curriculum at a "normal" rate. But it is a big mistake to identify learning ability with curriculum acquisition. . . . We need to conceive of learning more broadly and to recognize that it is an ongoing life process. Once we acknowledge that children are learning something all the time even if it is not what we set out to teach them—then we have considerably broadened our options for reaching children and for directing their mental growth."[1] We cannot guarantee what children learn from reading fiction, we can only assume that they learn something. With involvement in a substantial amount of reading, any child will absorb language and gradually, on their own terms, ingredients for survival. In the foreword to the book, TRIUMPHS OF THE HUMAN SPIRIT IN CHILDREN'S LITERATURE, Marcia Brown is quoted as saying, "It is hard to say just what effect the books we read in childhood have on our later life, but we all know they do have an effect—in images that will not be erased, in people as real as those we know, in conversations heard as echoes. . . ."[2]

Aidan Chambers, in a quote earlier in the text, spoke of "matters of the spirit," while the volume quoted above sought books which reflected the "triumph of the human spirit." In surveying the swath of materials read for this listing, it became clear that some authors have the ability to present salient characters in stories which give us hope about the nature of humans. Hearing or feeling the "echoes" from such titles can provide resources for survival at unknown and unexpected times in the lives of children. Several of such titles are reviewed here. Among others which resound pleasantly or poignantly in this author's memory are RABBLE STARKY by Lois Lowry for creative use of names—Rabble, the nickname for Parable Ann—and for the characters which epitomize strength to match the naming; THE GOATS by Brock Cole which places two young persons in the humiliating situation of being the outcasts (goats) at camp. The two awkwardly but stalwartly rise above their situation and discover much about life, survival, and closeness in their escape from the camp; and UNCLAIMED TREASURES by Patricia MacLachlan, in which the scenes of elders playing music in the yard and matter-of-factly dealing with death are unusual, as well as the story of adolescent growth which accompanies these scenes. The power of these stories is in the presentation of schematics reflecting a considerable range of the human circumstance.

This section of the text considers the four topics: People and the Environment, Religion and Politics, War and Peace, and Celebration of Life and Death as issues in children's novels. As more schools are beginning to include enviromental problems in the curriculum, non-fiction books which deal with planetary concerns are readily available. Fiction with focus on environmental themes is more difficult to find. With the increasing demand from schools, more titles may soon appear. For the youngest readers, numerous picture books have always offered sympathetic portrayals of animals. These, in some part, endorse the care and feeding of our fellow creatures, while not necessarily being directed toward environmental issues. Because of their prevalence, only a few samples of picture books which suggest an appreciation of nature are noted in our listing.

Noted are a few novels for middle to older readers, in which enviromental issues were found as the background for characterization and/or plot. While there is no substitute for factual information about the environment, good fiction could assist in planting clues in the minds and imaginations of children concerning the kind of world in which they wish to live.

Equally difficult to find were fiction materials which could assist young people in gaining a wider view of their world—culturally, socially, and politically. As was acknowledged earlier, children may be more concerned with the more immediate aspects of their lives such as home, school, peers and family—but preparation for later studies and understanding cannot ignore broader aspects of the child's world. For some uncanny reason, as American communities become more culturally diverse—and as the world becomes smaller through telecommunication, economic, and political patterns—children's fiction shows no similar broadening of focus. Books of non-fiction and folklore offer many more opportunities for children to gain an appreciation of other cultures and places in the world, than can be found in fiction. Here, we consider views of other peoples and societies in the section on politics, since it is the political notions of a nation which often influence or control access to world views. Admittedly, problems of publishing in other parts of the world, and problems in translation, contribute to the lack of availability of materials written by authors from many parts of the world, but the limited fictional representation of diverse populations within our own borders remains unexplained.

Both politics and religion are sometimes illusive issues, especially for children, but young readers can identify with characters who may be embroiled in political or religious circumstances as part of setting and plot. Unconcerned about implications for their adult lives, the memory of a particular character facing problems at a particular time, and in a particular place, may become ingrained in young psyches. Relating the novel to real life situations for some will come later, while realistically, children are the sons and daughters of politicians, activists, and preachers, and many of the books included in this section portray like circumstances. Political and religious decisions made by adults also affect the lives of many children. A few of our inclusions reflect such decisions. Noted also are a few historical novels which expose the politics affecting characters at a particular time in history. Children may not realize the intricacies of political systems, but they can understand that systems of power and decision making cause changes in the lives of book characters. Therefore, political issues need not be as illusive as sometimes claimed.

For adolescents, questions about political and religious issues often surface along with their personal introspection. They are ready to examine these issues in the light of their own lives and that of others. Adolescent exposure to a variety of political and religious thought may therefore be essential to their ability to formulate adult decisions in these areas—and most importantly, in their ability to respect the decisions made by others.

Fictional materials for children, which deal with the world's major wars are fairly abundant. Issues surrounding these wars are covered from many points of view. Peace, as an issue for human survival, is most often explored through coverage of the mechanisms of war. Messages about peace are made clear through the characterizations of those who have suffered through wars and the aftermath of wars. This is particularly true of books presenting personal accounts of the Holocaust, Hiroshima, and The Vietnam War. The issue of human suffering as a result of war is sometimes countered by titles which assume militaristic attitudes. American authors deal more often with the peripheral circumstances of war, rather than the hard-hitting life and death issues of war and peace—perhaps because the American continent has been spared from major wars since The Civil War. Because of the lack of real experience in war, some author's accounts are reportorial or contrived. Those close to the tragedy of wars have sometimes been reluctant to open the wounds of their experience in writing, and especially in writing for children. In her essay titled, "Why Would a Child Want to Read About That? The Holocaust Period in Children's Literature," Ursula Sherman ends by saying, "There may still exist a kind of old-fashioned shame about uncomfortable realities that makes adults say 'not in front of the children!' But this has not protected children from the real world. Adult secrecy may have shielded grown-ups from the naive and straightforward questions our young know how to pose, but in the long run our shameful secrets have become known even to children. The more our young know about why the Holocaust happened, and how it took place, the more they, as our future adults, will be prepared to deal with the trends in society that endanger our humanity."[3] Perhaps we should add that the more children learn about the possibilities of peace, the more likely it will be that we can find means, other than war, to solve the problems of the world.

The section on Celebration of Life and Death proposes that survival in life demands opportunities for celebration. It is in our celebration of the rhythms of nature, the sounds of the city and country, joys in successes and failures, hope in small things and appreciation of big things, which provide children with coping mechanisms. Festive occurrences complete with exhilerating illustrations are often portrayed in picture books directed to the very young. For this reason, I advocate the use of picture books with much older audiences than those for which they were intended. Included are several examples, but many more are readily available. In addition, a few titles are listed in which the central characters show a zest for living even as adversities and problems are encountered.

The best of the books on death and dying are those which at the same time celebrate living. For example, GOODBYE GRANDPA, celebrates the relationship betweeen the grandfather and child before he dies and even after, when the child opens a letter addressed to him from his grandfather. An example for older readers is BREADSTICKS AND BLESSING PLACES, in which the central character learns to celebrate the life of her lost friend—and in this way ameliorates grief. In conclusion, the words of Walter Dean Myers seem appropriate: "Let us celebrate the children—the singers and the silent, the brave and the frightened, the newly born and the fallen angels. Those who hold their pain and silent grief, and those who rage back at us. . . . Let us hear the questions in their tears, and let us hear them with our hearts. . . . In the beginning, let us celebrate the children, and bring them peace, and, in the end let us celebrate the children and bring them peace."[4]

NOTES

1. Elkind, David, *Children and Adolescents. Interpretive Essays on Jean Piaget.* p. 99. New York: Oxford University Press, 1970.

2. Foreword by Marcia Brown in, *Triumphs of the Spirit in Children's Literature,* edited by Francelia Butler and Richard Rotert. p. xi. Library Professional Publications, © 1986.

3. Sherman, Ursula F., "Why Would a Child Want to Read about That? The Holocaust Period in Children's Literature," in *How Much Truth Do We Tell the Children? The Politics of Children's Literature,* edited by Betty Bacon. p. 182. Minneapolis, Minn.: MEP Publications, © 1988.

4. Myers, Walter Dean, "Let Us Celebrate the Children," in *Horn Book Magazine,* Jan./Feb. 1990, p.47. Adapted from the author's acceptance speech for the 1989 Coretta Scott King Award for his book, *Fallen Angels,* delivered at the American Library Association, June 27, 1989.

III. VIEWS OF THE WORLD

People and the Environment

ANIMAL MOTHERS by Atsushi Komori. Illus. by Masayuki Yabuuchi. New York: Philomel Books, 1983. Youngest-Younger

Love of animals can be promoted through this book showing animal mothers taking care of their young. The simple text is accompanied by strong, realistic, illustrations. Others by this team are available.

CLEMENTINA'S CACTUS by Ezra Jack Keats. Illus. by the author. New York: Viking Press, 1982. Youngest

Keats portrayal of a young girl walking through the desert with her father will help young people appreciate the beauty of the desert. The wordless story is accompanied by humorous, old-fashioned illustrations. A blooming cactus indicates the beauty to be found in the desert.

DOWNWIND, by Louise Moeri. New York: Dutton, 1984. Middle-Older

Ephraim Dearborn and his family face frightening events, which those who live near nuclear power plants hope will never happen. An announcement on radio informs everyone that an accident has occurred, and that the nuclear plant could experience a meltdown. The Isla Coneja plant is only thirty miles upwind from the community where the Dearborn's and others live. If the meltdown happens, deadly radiation could cover their valley.

Most of this rather compelling story covers the family's attempt to escape, "downwind." They face mounting hysteria, panic, and the resulting violence. The highways are jammed and tempers are raw.

Taut exciting reading is provided as the Dearborns manage their escape, while enduring their fears, and the complications of little sister, Jocelyn, being injured.

This is good writing but it is also one of the few books for children which deals with this particular environmental issue.

DRIFT by William Mayne. New York: Delacorte, 1985. Middle-Older

Rafe's mother doesn't want him to talk to the "heathen" Indian girl who lives in the north country village encampment of tents and cabins. Rafe finds himself intrigued with the girl, and her knowledge of the bear, which she speaks of in human terms. He follows the girl on a trip, and ends up afloat on an island of ice which has broken away. An interesting story of communication with animals in the wild.

THE DYING SUN by David Blackwood New York: Atheneum, 1989. Oldest

Set not far into the future, about 2050, this story places a young boy named James in the Western Hemisphere, after the ice age has begun to return. Many North Americans have moved south seeking warmth. The beginning of the story places James and his family across the border in Mexico where they live in crowded, slum conditions. The Mexican Liberation Army threatens the lives of the "gringos" who have crowded into their territory. James's family decides to leave and move North, where they will try to find a way to survive in Missouri. James refuses to go, but later changes his mind. A good portion of the story describes events during James's trip North and the family's struggles in the North Country.

The story is told in first person, which does not work well, in this case, for setting the background to the story. No descriptions of how this all happened are offered, making the scientific possibilities of the cooling of the sun almost trite. The Mexican gangs are unable to describe their feelings about the intrusions on their lives so their actions appear almost gratuitous and stereotypical. The story is somewhat redeemed by the events placed in the North Country. The struggles there seem based in reality. This book could be used to introduce the environmental issues relating to pollution and the sun, but should be used with non-fiction providing more information.

HAIRLINE CRACKS by John Taylor. New York: Dutton (Lode-star), 1990. Older

Couched in a mystery, concerns about the problems of nuclear waste disposal are voiced. The story begins with the mysterious disappearance of Sam's mother and subsequently the disappearance of her friend, Davis, a journalist. Unable to get any information, except a coded message which arrives in the mail, Sam and his friend Mo set out to uncover the whereabouts of the two. They have few clues, but manage to uncover the truth. A local business-man wishes to build housing on land which has been declared unsafe, because of its proximity to an old nuclear waste storage facility. There is some excitement in the mystery, although much seems contrived including the characterization of the culprit. The nuclear waste issue is not prominent in the story, but becomes evident near the end. The writing is shallow, but the book may be useful in arousing interst in the subject of nuclear waste and other waste disposal problems.

A HOME IS TO SHARE . . . AND SHARE . . . AND SHARE by Judie Angell. Scarsdale, New York: Bradbury, 1984. Middle

When the town's animal shelter is closed, a family of children busy themselves seeking support from the community and finding shelter for abandoned animals.

THE HUNTER AND THE ANIMALS by Tomie de Paola. Illus. by the author. New York: Holiday House, 1981. Youngest

A wordless picture book tells the story of a hunter who changes his mind about hunting animals. After realizing that animals are his friends, the hunter breaks his gun.

LET A RIVER BE by Betty Sue Cummings. New York: Atheneum, 1978. Older-Oldest

The author presents marvelous characterizations and an ex-traordinary sense of place in this environmental novel. The river is important to Ella, an aged woman who lives on the fish she can catch, eat, and sell. Her home by the river is the place where she lived with her beloved husband, Doc, before he died. There, Ella feels she can hear his voice and sometimes even feel his touch. She has become something of outcast, in the area, because of her fight to save the river from pollution. She rides about town with signs on the back of her tricycle admonishing others to join her in the fight—but development proceeds and the river suffers. Many of the inhabitants of the water have already disappeared, and now the remaining fish are threatened by proposals for new housing along the river banks. Sometimes feeling alone in her fight for existence and her fight to save the river, Ella, encounters the "wild man" being hunted by the locals. He is smelly, frightened, and hungry. Ella, who meant only to feed him and send him on his way, finds herself attached to the young man who calls himself "Reetard." She befriends and houses the young "wild " man and finds that he is slow to learn, but far from crazy. Somewhere in his past, mistreatment has contributed to his slowness.

With Ella, the young man develops a zest for living. He assists her with her life near the river and grows into a character liked by most who meet him. Life for Ella is more complete, and the boy has at last found a "mama." The two join forces to save the river, and in the latter scenes of the book, the young man called "Reetard" gives his life in that effort.

This title emphasizes commitment to a cause, zest for living, and sympathy for creatures in and around the river. Questions are posed about "progress" and "development" being more environmentally destructive than rewarding. The loving relationship which develops between Ella and Reetard is a memorable one.

NATURE WALK by Douglas Florian. Illus. by the author. New York: Greenwillow, 1989. Youngest

One among many "appreciation of nature books" for the very young. The author of A SUMMER DAY now takes children on a late spring walk in the woods. With color illustrations of the scenery, cartoonlike illustrations of a boy and an older female are added. Children are coaxed to experience language with old style rhymes such as, "On the Trail Cottontail." Twenty plants and animal are pictured and listed at the end. Readers are encouraged to find them in the book.

NOAH'S SPACESHIP by Brian Wildsmith. Illus. by the author. New York: Oxford University Press, 1980. Younger

An enviromental message is present in this fanciful title for the young. Sometime in the future, animals begin to notice changes—food is hard to find, the air is foul and eggs are so fragile they break before hatching, When the animals consult Professor Noah, he invites them to join the spaceship and they travel for forty days and forty nights to a place where they can find the beauty they once had on their planet before it became polluted. They travel back in time to the original earth. The story line is sparse, but the pictures are good and add enough to the story to make this a worthwhile enviromental piece reminiscent of the Bible story of Noah.

ON THE FAR SIDE OF THE MOUNTAIN by Jean Craighead George. Illus. by the author. New York: Dutton, 1990. Middle-Older

More than thirty years later, the story Of Sam Gribley is resumed shortly after it ended in MY SIDE OF THE MOUNTAIN. Vivid pictures of life in the wild are offered in this less than satisfying novel about black market bird dealers. The descriptions of the wilderness are still outstanding.

ONLY FIONA by Beverly Keller. New York: Harper and Row, 1988. Middle

Celebrating a child with real committment to life and joyfully touting animal rights, this is the story of Fiona Foster, who has just moved to a new town. While establishing and developing friendships in her new setting, Fiona is dedicated to protecting all animals.
There are hilarious escapades with Fiona protecting an ant hill, saving a beetle from a spider web, rescuing a bee from a wedding bouquet, and mounting a campaign to save the fish in a tank at the dentist's office.

SEAL CHILD by Sylvia Peck. Illustrated by Robert Andrew Parker. New York: Morrow, 1989. Middle-Older

This strange and irresistible story is based on Scottish legend and it gracefully fuses fact and fantasy. During winter, Molly and her family visit their island vacation cottage in Maine. Molly spends loving moments with an elderly neighbor, Ruby, who tells her enchanting stories about the seals which inhabit the island waters. During a walk on the beach, Molly discovers a dead mother seal, killed and skinned by drunken marauders. In the water she hears the haunting cries of a baby seal. Soon thereafter, a little girl named Maera appears. Molly notices Maera's pale complexion, the thin red marks on her face, her endurance of the cold, and her strikingly blue eyes. Maera will swim in the pool, but never in the ocean and, later, Molly realizes that like the selkie legends, this is a seal-child, who can never swim in the ocean, unless she wishes to change again to a seal. Information about seals is integrated into this story of enchantment which should capture the minds and hearts of many readers, as Ruby's words captured Molly, "I've seen their tears though some say its only seawater. You don't want to see one cry, though, it would break your heart to look into those eyes."

THE TALKING EARTH by Jean Craighead George. New York: Harper and Row, 1983. Middle-Older

Appreciation of people who respect the environment, wildlife and animals can be gained through this story about Billie Wind, a Seminole Indian girl who goes to live in the Florida Everglades, to discover the "roots" of her tribe's ancient beliefs. The contrivance of the situation does not detract from Billie's story of survival. Environmental messages may be a little too strong and the ending is less than satisfying. Marred but useful.

A TIME TO FLY FREE by Stephanie S. Tolan. New York: Charles Scribner's, 1983. Middle

This story is of a young boy who doesn't like school. He's tired of his teachers giving him work he already knows and he is tired of pretending to be like the other children. His real love is animals and other things. He speaks with the language of a precocious ten year old and, one day, Josh simply walks out of school.

During this time, Josh finds Rafferty, who lives nearby and has his own hospital for sick birds. Some of the birds live and some don't but Josh is fascinated enough to try some environmental action on his own which almost ends in disaster.

In the end, his parents—especially his mother—realize his plight and seek alternative methods of schooling for Josh.

TUCKER by Tom Birdseye. New York: Holiday House, 1990. Middle-Older

For discussions of hunting versus the preservation of animals, this book will add new dimensions. The story is of Tucker, an eleven-year-old who dreams of being an Indian warrior and capturing his first deer. The dream smolders while another part of his life is dealt with. With the visit of his nine-year-old sister, dreams that his divorced parents will reconcile intrude. These two elements aggravate turmoil in Tucker's life as he moves closer to his warrior dream. It is the event of his first kill which stands out most starkly in the story. Tucker finds the actual killing a lot less satisfying than he had dreamed. His tears are for the dead deer, and for himself, the hunter and disappointed child.

WAVEBENDER: A STORY OF DANIEL AU FOND by Tom
    Shachtman. Illus. by Jamichael Henterly. New York: Henry
    Holt and Co., 1989. Older

    Shachtman uses a sea lion named Daniel au Fond to introduce readers to life in the sea. Adventures of the seal were begun in his first book, BEACHMASTER. Daniel's exploits at sea realistically introduce readers to other sea creatures.

WHO WILL SPEAK FOR THE LAMB? by Mildred Ames. New
    York: HarperCollins, 1989. Older

    In spite of the author's attempts to add "flavor" to this story about animal rights, the heavy-handed message fails as a novel. Julie Peters, a former New York teen model moves to California where her first friends are animal rights activists, while Julie's father uses animals in scientific experimentation. Readers are introduced to Julie's problems with her family but the characterizations are shallow and the overall strength of the story does not match the sensational scene in the prologue, where a lamb is slaughtered in a high school biology class, with complete gory details.

WILLY CAN COUNT by Anne Rockwell. Illus. by the author.
    New York: Little, Brown and Co. (Arcade), 1989. Youngest

    This title can be used with other books on nature walks. It also presents a small child's sense of celebration about his ability to count which is the books real purpose. Using bright watercolors, Rockwell pictures Willy and his mother on a walk. Mother identifies objects for Willie, while Willie discovers even more things to count, including ladybugs.

III. VIEWS OF THE WORLD

Religion and Politics

ANNA TO THE INFINITE POWER by Mildred Ames. New
York: Charles Scribner's, 1981. Older-Oldest

Cloning is a current political topic and may become even more
controversial in the future. This unusual book set sometime in the
1990s presents this issue. Anna's brother, Rowan Hunt, has always
thought that she was cold and unemotional. Anna and the family
learn the shocking information that Anna's differences may be due
to the fact that she was cloned. Anna's mother, a scientist, explains
her willingness to participate in, and her pride in, the results of this
experiment. Anna is the clone of a famous female scientist, and
according to her mother, there are other Annas who were part of
the same experiment.

Rowan enlists the help of a teacher, Michaella Dupont, to help
humanize Anna. Serious questions are posed about choices for the
future.

AN ARABIAN HOME: LEILA AND MUSTAPHA'S STORY by
Christina Balit. Illus. by the author. New York: Watts, 1988.
Younger-Middle

A festive look at Arabian culture when Leila, thirteen and
Mustapha, ten leave an Arabian city to spend several days in the
desert. They have traveled to the desert to attend a cousin's
wedding. Mustapha and his cousin Rashid go falconing and visit
a camel-herding uncle, who gives them milk fresh from the camels.
The boys join the men in the wedding festivities, while Leila
and her mother stay at camp. The women prepare for the wedding
with the other womenfolk and attend only the "women's wedding."

Nicely illustrated with color- and black-and-white collages, the story offers information about another culture in a nonjudgemental way.

THE BELIEVERS by Rebecca C. Jones. New York: Little, Brown and Co. (Arcade), 1989. Older

Tibby is drawn to a fundamentalist religious sect, because of her relationship to Berl, a member, and because of her own life situation. Tibby is an adopted child, but finds no love at home because her adoptive mother, a TV reporter, is too busy to care. Seeking solace, Tibby becomes involved in the realistically portrayed fervor of the sect.

BEYOND SAFE BOUNDARIES by Margaret Sacks. New York: Lodestar, 1989. Older-Oldest

Political issues are explicit in this novel about Elizabeth Levin, growing up in South Africa. Her privileged family is viewed in the first few pages, where scenes with servants, education at a private school, and a new stepmother are the focus. It is when Elizabeth's sister goes to college and becomes involved with a student leader of mixed race that the political atmosphere is exposed.

Some information is provided about the plight of Blacks in South Africa, through the characterizations of servants, but little is seen of the real situation of Blacks. Whites, Jews, and Colored are the populations with whom the book is primarily concerned. Classroom and/or library discussions of the politics of South Africa would need evidence of all points of view, making this an important story.

CHILD OF WAR by Mary Ann Sullivan. New York: Holiday House, 1984. Older-Oldest

The conflicts in Northern Ireland represent one of the more vivid modern examples of the antagonism which can result from religious and political differences. In this tragic story, the contention is seen through the eyes of a young Catholic girl, who retreats into fantasy as the tensions of war become too much for her. Her parents are fighting for the IRA. (Also useful for the topic War and Peace)

CIRCLE OF FIRE by William H. Hooks. New York: Margaret K. McElderry, 1983. Middle-Older

Two boys, one Black and one White, and both eleven years old, become involved in saving a band of Irish tinkers from a planned attack of the KKK. Set in 1936, the issues surrounding racism and the practices of the KKK were social, religious and political. Although this story does not clearly point out such issues, they are implicit in confrontations which result. There is irony in the accurate fact that two boys of different races could be friends in spite of this.

DECEMBER SECRETS by Patricia Reilly Giff. Illus. by Blanche Sims. New York: Yearling Books, 1984. Younger

An easy to read story about friends giving presents during Christmas and Hanukkah. Compares both religious rituals for young children.

THE DEVIL IN VIENNA by Doris Orgel. New York: Dial, 1978. Older

This award winning story deals with the politics of Naziism before WW II. Issues of religion are obvious as the story deals with friends, one Christian and one Jewish. The changes in the daily lives and relationships of Jewish children in Vienna will be understood and with a little assistance most readers could relate the story to the politics causing such changes.

JUMP SHIP TO FREEDOM by James Collier and Christopher Collier. New York: Delacorte, 1981. Older

Historical political processes which affected the lives of Blacks in America are apparent in this novel about a young slave, Daniel Arabus. Set during the United States Constitutional Convention, Daniel meets George Washington, Alexander Hamilton and others. Although Daniel gains his freedom, the political systems which affect other Blacks are still in place, and others evolve, such as the fugitive slave law. Notes and background information are given at the end.

These authors have penned two other titles in a trilogy of forthright views of the lives of Blacks during this period. The other titles are WAR COMES TO WILLY FREEMAN and WHO IS CARRIE?

THE LONG NIGHT WATCH by Ivan Southhall. New York: Farrar, Straus and Giroux, 1983. Older-Oldest

Based in fact, this is the story of a religious group, who during World War II, set out from Australia to an island called Tangu Tangu to await the end of the world and the second coming of God. The "end" comes in a way surprising to the characters and to readers.

A LONG WAY TO GO by Zibby O'Neal. Illus. by Michael Dooling. New York: Viking (Once Upon America Series), 1990. Middle-Older

A wealthy New York City household is disrupted when ten-year-old Lila's wealthy grandmother is arrested while picketing the White House for women's suffrage. The year is 1917. World War I is in progress, and members of Lila's household resent her grandmother's actions. Lila, frustrated by her own situation at home, supports her grandmother and joins in a march for women's suffrage. The author makes some tame attempts to show her character's concern for the impoverished side of America but the strength of this story is its presentation of a historical event relating to women's suffrage. The story might have more impact used with A TIE TO THE PAST by David Weisman, which also deals with the suffragette movement but in more detail. The protagonist of the latter finds the diary of Gladys Mayhew, a protester on the London scene.

A MATTER OF SPUNK by Adrienne Jones. New York: Harper and Row, 1983. Middle-Older

Set in the pre-depression era of the twenties, this book combines humor with some of the eerie situations that develop when a mother and daughter make their home in a theosophical colony. The trip to California, the setting in the Hollywood Hills, and the colorful characterizations combine for an effective story.

MORNING GLORY AFTERNOON by Irene Bennett Brown. New York: Atheneum, 1982. Older-Oldest

Grieving and feeling guilt after her boyfriend's accidental death, Jessy Faber moves away from the family ranch to work in town as a switchboard operator. She restores her self esteem by exposing the activities of the KKK. The story is set during the early twenties, in Kansas. In addition to presenting the political extremes of the KKK, the story evokes a good sense of time and place.

MY MOTHER IS THE SMARTEST WOMAN IN THE WORLD
by Eleanor Clymer. Illus. by Nancy Kincade. New York:
Atheneum, 1982. Younger

A child-sized view of politics is offered in this story of
Kathleen, whose mother is running for mayor.

THE NINTH ISSUE by Dallin Malmgren. New York: Delacorte,
1989. Older

Much fuel for discussion of political issues is available in this
story concerned primarily with the topic of intellectual freedom.
Set in a high school in San Antonio Texas, eight student staff
members and their advisor, Mr. Choate publish the school newspaper. Each chapter in the book covers the publishing of one issue of
the paper. While insight is given to the lives and times of the
students, tension develops at its highest when the paper exposes the
fact that a passing grade has been arranged for one of the school's
star football players. Mr. Choate has encouraged the young people
to write about matters of choice, while warning them about fairness.
The controversy leads to his termination but the students work for
his reinstatement. Thus, the politics surrounding freedom of
expression, sports, and fairness in employment are issues which
arise in this well written novel.

PEOPLE MIGHT HEAR YOU by Robin Klein. New York:
Viking, 1987. Older

An unusual title dealing with mind control and religious
fanaticism. Frances is uneasy from the beginning about her surrogate mother's marriage to Mr. Tyrell, but she looks forward to a real
home, after years of apartment living. After the marriage takes
place, with limited ceremony, Frances soon discovers that she is
confined to the house, along with Tyrell's daughters. She and the
other residents live behind a wall, and are instructed never to leave
the house. When Frances is taken out, on only one occasion, it is
because she has serious dental problems. Even then, her real name
cannot be revealed to the dentist. This arrangement is seriously
disturbing for a free-thinking child like Frances.

"Aunt" has been the only mother Frances has ever known and
Frances struggles to conform to the regimens of the strange sect of
which they have become a part. Aunt ignores all problems for the
sake of the security offered her by Mr. Tyrell. Tyrell's daughters

have fallen under the spell of conformity, except for one who in the end joins Frances in her desperate attempt to escape.

THE PREACHER'S BOY by Terry Pringle. Chapel Hill, N.C.: Algonquin Books, 1988. Oldest

Beginning with a hilarious scene of a preacher's son, still in high school, attempting to preach his first sermon, but instead dissolving into uncontrollable laughter, the author presents a humorous yet complex novel about growing up and religious choice.

Michael Page, the preacher's son, spends his senior year trying to sort out his feelings about faith, his father's expectations, and love. During this time, he develops a relationship with Amy Hardin which is compellingly and gratuitously sexual. Even in this relationship, Michael is torn between the demands of his body and visions of eternal damnation.

When Michael goes to college, he becomes involved in more exploits, away from the likelihood of intrusion from his father, but the confrontation between father and son does occur in the end.

Although the religious issues are central to the story, this book is sexually explicit and definitely for mature readers.

THE RABBI'S GIRLS by Johanna Hurwitz. Illus. by Pamela Johnson. New York: William Morrow and Co., 1982. Middle

A family story which realistically approaches the subjects of religious prejudice and intolerance.

A RAG, A BONE, AND A HANK OF HAIR by Nicholas Fisk. New York: Crown, 1980. Older

Sometimes science fiction novels present plots alluding to political and social issues. This one is included as only one example. Brian is one of those who populates a community of controlled social planning. His desire for freedom of choice forms the basis for action.

THE RETURN by Sonia Levitin. New York: Atheneum, 1987. Older- Oldest

In this novel about Ethiopian Jews, Desta, a young girl, leaves Ethiopia with her brother hoping to immigrate to Israel. The Jews of Ethiopia are outcasts from their own people and are often mistreated in their struggle for existence as a religious minority. A glossary and bibliography append the novel.

RICE WITHOUT RAIN by Minfong Ho. New York: Lothrop, Lee and Shepard 1990. Older-Oldest

Set in Thailand, this novel presents political issues and views of another culture. Jinda's father, Inthorn, is encouraged by visiting students from Bangkok to resist making his land rent payment. He is jailed and dies in prison. Jinda joins in student rallies for the farmers and is attracted to Ned, one of the student dissenters. The author apparently writes with an informed view, providing readers with details about Thailand and Thai culture.

THE ROAD TO MEMPHIS by Mildred Taylor. New York: Dial, 1990. Older-Oldest

Inclusively, all of Taylor's books are political as they expose the plight of Black people in a society where political and social stuctures have historically impacted negatively on their lives and progress. The setting here is Mississippi in 1941, and although the impending war has created some job opportunities for Blacks, discrimination and racism are still blatant. The focus is on Cassie, now seventeen years old, her brother Stacey, and their friends, who are confronted and often humiliated by the white people they encounter. In one pivotal scene, a young man who defends himself after merciless taunting realizes he must leave Mississippi rather than face an unfair "justice " system. During that escape to Memphis, the friends face even more racist situations. Evidence of political and social oppression is more harshly apparent in this story than in Taylor's earlier titles which emphasized family strengths.

SHABANU; DAUGHTER OF THE WIND by Suzanne Fisher Staples. New York: Alfred A. Knopf, 1989. Older

Shabanu is the younger daughter in a family of nomadic camel herders. Life in the Cholistan desert of modern Pakistan is not easy, but Shabanu is proud of her way of life while aware that nomads are viewed with hatred by some. Being almost twelve years old, tradition dictates that a marriage will soon be arranged for the young girl. Shabanu's father arranges marriages for her and for her older sister Phulan. Sudden events affect their lives. Phulan's bridegroom is murdered, on the eve of their wedding—and Phulan is hurriedly married to Shabanu's betrothed, leaving Shabanu to marry a wealthy older man with three other wives. Disappointed and distressed, Shabanu attempts to run away, but is unsuccessful. An engrossing story for older readers which provides information about a different way of life.

SISTERS, LONG AGO by Peg Kehret. New York: Dutton (Cobblehill Books), 1990. Middle-Older

This poignant story presents questions about beliefs and about truth as it follows the intense developments in the life of a Willow Paige, an adolescent girl. Willow has experienced dreams about herself being another person named Kalo, and she remembers a strange phrase from her dreams spoken in a different language. These dreams are vivid in her recollection as she follows the ordinary patterns of adolescent life—school, friends, awareness of males, and sibling rivalries. Sibling confrontations for Willow are complicated by the fact that her younger sister, Sarah, suffers from leukemia.
One day at the beach when Willow nearly drowns, she experiences a flashback which convinces her that she has lived another life. Her flashback also presents her with visions of her dead grandmother and grandfather, indicating their existence in another life. When she is saved from drowning by a young girl on the beach, Willow believes that her rescuer is the reincarnation of her sister from the past—the one she has seen in her dreams.
These experiences and subsequent dreams present Willow with questions about life, death, and reincarnation, just at the time that Sarah's remission from leukemia fails and her sister is hospitalized. Willow seeks for answers at a library lecture on reincarnation, where she meets a woman who explains the phenomena. Bathed in the "white light" of her new discovery, Willow attempts to heal her sister. When Sarah later dies, Willow's search for answers becomes much more complex. By this time, Willow has learned to accept the differing beliefs of her friend, Grechen, as worthy of consideration in her quest for truths about the meaning of life and death. Her quest helps her to cope with the loss of Sarah.

SPIRIT ON THE WALL by Ann O'Neal Garcia. New York: Holiday House, 1982. Middle-Older

Set in the Upper Paleolithic Period, this is a very well written story of family. Although the setting, beliefs and customs are ancient, the lessons of human interaction and conflict are universal.

When Mat Maw is born with crooked legs, her mother wants the child to be killed as is the custom, but grandmother, Em, saves the deformed baby from death and takes Mat Maw to live in her cave. In the cave, Em nourishes and loves her grandchild, massaging her legs daily until they become straighter.

Alienated from the rest of the family because she has saved this non-perfect child, Em teaches Mat Maw the ways of the tribes. The child's only other company is her brother, the cave painter. From him, Mat Maw learns the art of cave "writing" although this position is usually reserved for males. The "writing" is one of the sacred arts of the tribe.

The three, Em, Mat Maw, and her brother eventually have to flee the wrath of the tribe, when blamed for a disastrous occurrence. After settling with another tribe, Mat Maw faces the inevitable ageing and death of her grandmother. Tragically, she blames herself for having drawn the "spirit" image of her grandmother on a cave wall. Such visual representations are thought to cause death. Her brother helps Mat Maw to accept death without blame.

A SPIRIT TO RIDE THE WHIRLWIND by Athena V. Lord. New York: Macmillan, 1981. Middle-Older

The politics of worker's rights and unions has been dealt with in only a few books for children. This one looks at that subject historically through a story about life in Massachusetts in 1836. Twelve-year-old Binnie is involved in a strike at the mill. While on strike, her dreams of making enough money to improve her life will not materialize, but there is hope for Binnie from another source.

SPUD TACKETT AND THE ANGEL OF DOOM by Robbie Branscum. New York: Viking, 1983. Older

Spud Tackett has enjoyed life on his grandma's farm in the hills of Arkansas, until his city cousin comes to live with them. Spud resents the attention and deference given to his cousin by grandma. In spite of this, Spud and his cousin become companions.

The two boys are both intrigued when a high rolling preacher storms into town. The community surrounds the messenger with accolades, their money, and their food. Grandma is one of the few who is hesitant about the preacher's intentions. While he preaches hell, damnation, fire and brimstone, it is revealed that the preacher is a con man.

Family interactions provide an interesting view of a rural Arkansas community, and the antics of the preacher provide an unusual view of a religious con artist.

A STRING OF CHANCES by Phyllis Reynolds Naylor. New York: Atheneum, 1983. Older

Sixteen-year-old Evie, a minister's daughter spends the summer with her married cousin. When the cousin's new baby dies, Evie finds herself questioning her belief in God.

TANCY by Belina Hurmence. New York: Clarion, 1984. Oldest

After emancipation, Tancy leaves the plantation to search for her mother and to learn about the outside world. Because she can read, Tancy is employed by the Freedman's Bureau. Tancy's search for her mother, her work, and the decisions she has to make, provide readers with views of the social and political atmosphere during these times.

TUAN by Eva Boholm-Olsson. Pictures by Pham van Don. Translated by Dianne Jonasson. New York: Farrar, Straus and Giroux (R&S Books), 1986. Younger

A village story set in Vietnam, giving readers a view of everyday life and problems. The colorful illustrations are instructive and nicely drawn. Tuan is bitten by a dog, and has to take shots to prevent rabies. His circumstance indicates the shortage of necessities, when the doctor wonders if there will be enough medicine to finish the series of shots. The shots are completed and Tuan is able to join in the festivities of Children's Day.

WHAT HAPPENED TO HEATHER HOPKOWITZ? by Charlotte Herman. New York: E.P. Dutton, 1981. Older

Many elements of Orthodox Jewish traditions are explained in this story of a young girl who is absorbed in Orthodox rites in spite of her parents' differing views. While her parents are away on a cruise, Heather stays with an Orthodox family of friends. Through this exposure, Heather decides to change her life.

WHAT I REALLY THINK OF YOU by M.E. Kerr. New York:
Harper and Row, 1982. Older-Oldest

This novel offers an inside view of two families whose business
is religion. Opal is the only daughter of a Pentecostal preacher. Her
father runs The Helping Hand Tabernacle. Because Opal is
different, she is excluded from the rest of the crowd at school. Jesse
and his brother, Bud, are also preacher's children, but their father
has a lucrative television ministry. Through Opal and Jesse readers
are familiarized with the difficulties of growing up while being
different. Although there is the danger of generalities being drawn,
insights are given to religious family life and to the struggles and
hopes of children with ministers as parents. Their questions about
being different, their questions about their parents, their confusion
about religion, their hopes of having lives like other people, and
their struggles to believe are all evident.

WHEN THUNDERS SPOKE by Virginia Driving Hawk Sneve.
Illus. by Oren Lyons. New York: Holiday House, 1974.
Middle-Older

Conflicts between ancient beliefs and the ways of modern life
are seen in this brief story about a young man living on a reservation
in South Dakota. It is grandfather who continues to believe in the
old ways, while Norman Two Bull's mother is more attuned to the
new religion of the church nearby. For years, Norman has collected
agates and exchanged them for "candy" at the local trading post.
Now he is older and has needs and wants of his own. He soon
discovers that the agates which he has exchanged for candy are
worth money.

Grandfather sends Norman off to Thunder Butte, where the
boy finds a "coup" stick used in ancient times. Bringing the stick
home foments an argument between his father and mother. Their
concern is whether the stick represents Wakan (good), or is it
bringing the evil of superstitions and "heathen" ways into the home.
Events which follow allow Norman to make his own decisions about
what is good and bad. He confronts his own feelings about the new
and the old. In the end, Norman and his grandfather, together,
return the ancient stick to the earth.

This story not only confronts issues of belief, but also asks
questions about what is important in life. Economic growth, in
conflict with sacred beliefs, is blatantly questioned when Norman
is offered pay for leading tourists to the sacred site in search of

agates. When the white owner of the trading post proposes that Thunder Mountain be turned into a agate quarry, and when the storeowner offers a large amount of money to purchase the ancient stick, values are again at risk. Although this is a short book, the messages are not slight, making the story useful with much older readers than it appears.

WHICH WAY COURAGE by Eiveen Weiman. New York: Atheneum, 1981. Middle-Older

The need that some have to break away from strong religious traditions is explored in this story about an Amish girl named, Courage Kuntzler. Courage would like to continue her education even though tradition dictates that after finishing eighth grade she should marry. Concerns about her handicapped brother help her to make hard decisions.

THE WILDERNESS HAS EARS by Alice Wellman. New York: Harcourt Brace Jovanovich, 1975. Older

This book is included because it deals with a part of the world which is not often seen in children's books. It is set in the wilderness of Portuguese Angola. The book was written in 1975 when Angola first became free, and the author offers a plea for peaceful developments there. Elements of the narrative could provide the catalyst for discussions of present day Angola and its surroundings.

Luti, a European girl who lives in Angola, follows her guardian, Nduku, to his native village. Nduku has been attacked by a leopard and returns to his village for healing. Inside the Kimbutu village, Luti observes tribal rituals of healing. Her own acute sunburn is treated by Onavita the tribal healer. For some time, Luti awaits her father because Nduku is too sick to take her home. The healer Onavita takes Luti into her hut.

During Luti's stay, more views of healing rites are offered and the struggles of living during a period of drought are amplified. The chief is an educated person, who has traveled, studied, and returned to his village. Relief from the drought, is followed by tragedy when the rain finally falls but is followed by flash floods. Many of the tribe are killed including Onavita. It is Luti who rescues the "soulfire" of the tribe from Onavita's hut. With these fires still burning, the tribe's renewal will be possible.

THE WILLOW WHISTLE by Priscilla Homola. Illus. by Ted
Lewin. New York: Dodd Mead, 1983. Older

Elements of rural life, religion, and religious conflicts are dealt
with in this story of a young girl confronting her preacher father.
The characterizations are simplistic and reminiscent of the past, but
ingredients of young love will have appeal for some readers.

III. VIEWS OF THE WORLD

War and Peace

Selections concentrate on stories about the Vietnam War and a few titles relating to other wars. In the first edition of SURVIVAL THEMES . . . , a substantial list of materials on World War II is included.

AND ONE FOR ALL by Theresa Nelson. New York; Franklin Watts (Orchard Bks.), 1989. Older-Oldest

   A brief view of the peace movement during the Vietnam War era is offered in this story told by a teenage girl. Geraldine Brennan finds herself in love with her brother's best friend Sam. While growing up, Geraldine has been allowed to tag along on many of the boys' adventures including the day that they carved their names in Lover's Tree. Now, Sam and her brother Wing are seniors in high school and Geraldine secretly loves Sam in a different way. Tranquility is further disturbed by the fact that Wing has become rebellious and as a result, his grades have suffered.
   When the War in Vietnam becomes an issue, all hope that Sam and Wing will not be drafted because of their plans to enter college. Fearful that he will not graduate and angry at being barred from sports because of his grades, Wings joins the Marines. Sam becomes a leader in the peace movement.
   When Wing is killed in Vietnam, the family and Geraldine are angry with Sam and others who are demonstrating and promoting troop withdrawal from Vietnam. Geraldine travels to Washington where she confronts Sam, informing him of Wing's death. It is then that she understands— Sam's efforts were primarily for Wing.

BE EVER HOPEFUL HANNALEE by Patricia Beatty. New York: William Morrow and Co., 1980. Older

The story takes place in post Civil War Atlanta, where the reader is provided with a scenic view of the aftermath of war. Hannalee is working in a dry goods store to help her family survive, when her brother is arrested for a crime which he didn't commit. Hannalee sets out to find the real culprit and to clear her brother. A Black girl, whom she meets by chance, assists Hannalee in eventually finding the real criminal.

Just a cursory view of conflicts faced in the post Civil War South is offered in this story of family survival. However, the tragedy of war is evident and the story could be the catalyst for further study or discussion. Although Black characters are introduced, racial issues are not dealt with in detail. The attitudes expressed are necessarily from a Southern White point of view.

BLITZCAT by Robert Westall. New York: Scholastic, 1989. Older

The author of THE MACHINE GUNNERS has written an outstanding novel revealing the horrors of World War II. Set in England, the inventive plot follows a cat on its travels during the Blitz. The cat is never humanized, and the descriptions of the war are explicated through characters the cat meets in his search for his master. "Blitzcat" adds a special quality to the writing as his sequence of friends seem to have luck as result of their encounters with him. Historical events of the war are disclosed in vivid enthralling writing.

The earlier work, THE MACHINE GUNNERS is set in an English village during the war. Life amid the constant bombings is portrayed. The children make a game of collecting remnants from the war. One of them finds a machine gun around which much of the later action takes place.

A BOAT TO NOWHERE by Maureen Crane Cortski. Illus. by Dick Teicher. New American Library, 1980. Middle

A small family group travels from war torn Vietnam in a fishing boat, seeking safe haven from the war. Young readers are drawn closer to the plight of the boat people through the skillfully drawn characters and the hopelessness of their situation.

CHILDREN OF THE DUST by Louise Lawrence. New York: HarperCollins, 1985. Older

Will the human spirit find strength to survive the desolation of a nuclear holocaust? The book's cover with its huge mushroom cloud reveals the theme of this book, and the story is placed in England after the bombs have come. Out of the dust, a strange species has arisen. After the months and weeks of struggling for survival in a radiation ridden atmosphere, the survivors must consider what kind of world they will live in and develop.

CLEAR AND PRESENT DANGER by Tom Clancy. New York: Putnam, 1989. Oldest

The familiar author of novels of intrigue, chooses a current theme for this one. The plot involves several characters from past novels as the United States fights the drug war in Columbia. Action and suspense are woven around the drug agencies, the troops, and the individual agents who attempt to crush the drug lords.

CRUTCHES by Peter Hartling. Translated from German by Elizabeth D. Crawford. New York: Lothrop, Lee and Shepard 1988. Older-Oldest

Survival of World War II is seen from the point of view of a thirteen-year-old boy. Young Thomas Schramm, a supporter of Naziism, comes to Vienna after the war in search of his missing aunt. The details of his search reveal the destruction caused by the war. Scenes of his travels expose the situation of the homeless and the destitute. At a temporary shelter, the one-legged man, Crutches, appears. The two become attached to each other and travel together. Tom learns from Crutches and gradually recants his hatred of Jews. The power of this novel is in the vivid, unsparing, descriptions of human circumstance in the aftermath of war.

DECEMBER STILLNESS by Mary Downing Hahn. New York: Clarion/Houghton Mifflin, 1988. Older-Oldest

Modern day aftermath of war is dealt with in this novel in which Kelly fulfills a class assignment by interviewing the derelict who spends his days at the public library. She finds that the "bag man" is a Vietnam veteran who refuses to accept social services. The disturbed man wanders the streets suffering from post-traumatic stress as a result of the war.

Kelly sets out to save the man from himself, but instead the homeless veteran is killed in a car accident. In the background are

Kelly's parents who espouse the polarized attitudes of the sixties. Kelly fights constantly with her father over her grades, but after the traumatic accident she and her father, also a Vietnam veteran, make a pilgrimage to the Vietnam War Memorial in Washington, D.C.

THE ETERNAL SPRING OF MR. ITO by Sheila Garrigue. Scarsdale, N. Y., Bradbury Press, 1985. Middle-Older

Sara Warren lives in Vancouver, British Columbia. She loves the garden and finds special joy in her association with Mr. Ito, the Japanese gardener and his family. Mr. Ito gives her a bonsai of her own to nurture.

When America and Canada declare war on Japan, everything changes for the Ito family. Not only does the government impose separation and internment on the Japanese nationals, but Sara's family and friends turn away from those Japanese, whom they supposedly love and respect. The Warren family's resentment is compounded by the death of a cousin's husband-to-be, in the war.

Mr. Ito, a proud and sincere man, flees to the mountains to escape the shame of internment. Sara finds him there, and she promises to take a large bonsai, kept in her garage, to the Ito family.

After hiding the bonsai from members of her family who in their anger might destroy it, Sara carefully devises a plan. Managing to elude the authorities, she delivers the bonsai to the Itos at camp.

With the history, strength, and character of the Ito family symbolized by the aged bonsai plant, this is an intricate examination of the emotional conflicts of war. It offers a caring view of the trauma suffered by Japanese families during the World War II internment,—although told mostly from Sara's point of view. Use with LONE HEART MOUNTAIN by Ishigo for more of the Japanese point of view.

THE FORTY THIRD WAR by Louise Moeri. New York: Houghton Mifflin, 1989. Older-Oldest

Modern conflicts in another part of the world are detailed in this short novel set in Central America. At twelve years old, Uno Ramirez has been drafted into the revolutionary war. In an unknown place, easily reminiscent of El Salvador, the story follows Uno and his young cousin through their intensive training and in their first involvement in real fighting. After being exposed to Uno's circumstance, readers should come away from this book with questions about war as a process for solving national problems. The background of Uno's life of poverty, his father's death, and the seemingly unending series of wars are presented with strong messages, frank descriptions, and engrossing reading.

LISA'S WAR by Carol Matas. New York; Charles Scribner's Sons, 1989. Older-Oldest

Set in Copenhagen, in 1940, this is another story about the Danish resistance, told by an adolescent girl named Lisa. The story describes her participation in the resistance and the committment of her brother, while other members of the family refuse to become involved.

LONG TIME PASSING by Adrienne Jones. New York: Harper-Collins, 1990. Oldest

A picture of the peace movement of the sixties and of counter opinions are detailed in this novel set in Northern California. Twenty years later, Jonas revisits the scene and remembers the summer when he was eighteen. Conflicts, for Jonas, ran deep because his father was a marine in Vietnam, when he fell in love with peace activist, Auleen DeLange. Their story is poignantly remembered in a story about family, love and hard choices. In spite of his leanings toward the peace movement and his feelings for Auleen, Jonas's love for his father compelled him to join the marines.

LOS ALAMOS LIGHT by Larry Bogard. New York: Farrar, Straus and Giroux, 1983. Older-Oldest

New Mexico, during World War II, is the setting for this novel about a sixteen-year-old girl named Maggie. Readers learn about atomic bomb developments in that area, through Maggie's life on a secret government base. Details of life in the desert Southwest add a special flavor to the story.

A MONTH OF SEVEN DAYS by Shirley Climo. New York: HarperCollins (Crowell), 1987. Middle-Older

Twelve-year-old Zoe, lives with her mother and brother during the Civil War. Her father has gone off to war when the Yankees come and take over their home. Zoe learns that the

Yankee Captain is superstitious. This spawns an idea and Zoe develops a plan to get rid of the occupying troops.

Meantime, Zoe also strikes up an association with one of the young Yankee soldiers. She is surprised to find herself liking the young man very much. She finds that he is kind and good although he still remains the enemy.

In the end, Zoe's plan works, with a little assistance from her Indian friend, Mr. Hodge. More importantly, incidents which happen during "the occupation' have helped Zoe to grow in her perspectives of humanity. She knows that all "the enemy" are not bad. She learns not to be judgmental and not to make assumptions about others.

Superstition provides the humorous vehicle for this view of a southern family during the Civil War. The Indian, Mr. Hodge, is one of the least developed characters. He seems to be only introduced as scenic backdrop until he assists with Zoe's plan. His appearance in that situation is therefore almost startling. The rest of the story works much better.

MY HIROSHIMA by Junko Morimoto. New York: Viking Penguin, 1990. Middle-Older

Since Japan was the enemy, not many books for American children approach the subject of the destruction of Hiroshima. This picture story tells the story of Hunko Mirimoto as a child in Hiroshima. Her story of her own survival and that of her family is meant for younger readers but the cry for peace is meaningful to all.

NUMBER THE STARS by Lois Lowry. New York: Houghton Mifflin, 1989. Middle

Set in Copenhagen, this story celebrates the Danish resistance during World War II. When knowledge is received that the Germans plan to capture all Jews, life for Annemarie and her friend Ellen Rosen changes suddenly. Ellen's family seeks refuge elsewhere while Ellen is taken in by Annemarie's parents. Ellen is instructed that she will pose as a member of the Danish family. When the Germans appear inquiring about the whereabouts of the Rosen's, they notice that Ellen has dark hair while the other two children are blond. For one very tense moment, the two girls know fear as never before. Expertly, father solves the situation by showing the baby pictures of Annemarie's older sister, who has died and who luckily had dark hair when she very young.

Strategies used by the Danish underground in smuggling Jews out of Denmark to neutral Sweden are detailed as Ellen, her parents, and others are smuggled out, hidden in secret compartments of boats. Some members of the resistance were discovered and killed. One of those was a young man who was the fiance of Annemarie's sister Lise. Later in the story it is learned that Lise's death was also due to her participation in the resistance. Thousands of Jews were smuggled out of Denmark to safety in Sweden. The author provides notes at the end of the story stating that this is a fictionalized account of that story told to her by a friend.

POCKET CHANGE by Kathryn Jensen. New York: Bradbury, 1989. Older

Compared to DECEMBER STILLNESS (above), a haunting more personal story of post traumatic stress resulting from the Vietnam War is provided in this novel. Sixteen-year-old Josie Monroe's father is tortured by flashbacks of Vietnam killings. The trauma experienced by his wife and family are clearly detailed before the author turns the story to Josie's search for help. Readers are not provided with simple solutions. The beginning of the end comes only after Josie's father barricades himself in the house, and nearly shoots his own son. Only then does he realize how deeply his condition has deteriorated and agrees to seek help.

THE ROAD FROM HOME, THE STORY OF AN ARMENIAN GIRL by David Kherdian. New York: Greenwillow, 1979. Older

From a young Armenian girl's diary, the flight of Armenians from Turkey in 1915 is documented in novel form. This period of history is obscure for many, but the horrors as portrayed will be easy to compare with other eras.

THE SKY IS FALLING by Kit Pearson. New York: Viking, 1990. Middle-Older

Ten-year-old Norah's life, secure despite WW II, is changed drastically when she is evacuated to Canada with her five-year-old brother Gavin. There she changes from an outgoing child to a sullen bed wetter.

The wealthy widow and her spinster daughter with whom she lives show little understanding of her feelings. Norah attempts to run away, but finally accepts her situation.

This title could fit with others dealing with loneliness, in addition to assisting younger readers in discussions of peripheral spoils of war.

THE SLOPES OF WAR: A NOVEL OF GETTYSBURG by N.A. Perez. Houghton Mifflin, 1984. Older-Oldest

Interest in the Civil War has been spurred by the award-winning series on public broadcast television. Like the film series, this book bars no punches in describing the battle of Gettysburg. The Summerhill family are caught in the circumstance of having soldiers fighting on both sides of the conflict. In the Summerhill home casualties from both sides are cared for in different rooms. The children learn that no matter what one believes, war is not a pretty business. Substantial factual information is provided, while the story balances the human involvement.

A TIME TOO SWIFT by Margaret Poynter. New York: Atheneum, 1990. Older

Marjorie Ellison, fifteen years old, lives in San Siego in late 1941. Her story reveals the effects of WW II on Marjorie and her family. The story includes a romantic interest, loss of lives, and a reference to the relocation of the Japanese. Adolescent readers will relate to Marjorie, who is presented as a fairly typical adolescent with egocentric thoughts and actions.

THE WALL by Eve Bunting. Illus. by Ronald Himler. New York. Houghton Mifflin (Clarion), 1990. Younger-Oldest

Although designed for younger readers, the message is one which can be used with all ages. A father and his young son have come to the Vietnam Memorial to find the name of the grandfather the little boy never knew. The breadth of the war's destruction is seen in the characters reflected in the wall, all who have come for personal reasons to the memorial. The boy sees the reflection of himself and his father. He speaks to an amputee in a wheelchair, sees an old couple crying, and watches a class visiting the wall with their teacher. When grandpa's name is found, the boy and his father make a rubbing of it. They place the rubbing at the base of the memorial where many others have left tokens of their love. The book presents a moving portrayal for all ages in picture and story. Most poignant is the moment when a grandfather passes nearby taking a walk with his grandson.

WHERE THE ELF KING SINGS by Judie Wolkoff. New York: Bradbury, 1980. Older

To be used with other books on the Vietnam War and post-traumatic stress, this novel also deals with the mental pain suffered by Vietnam veterans after the war. Resulting family problems are again the catalyst for this plot about a teenage girl whose father is a Vietnam veteran suffering flashbacks. Marie's father has become an alchoholic because he cannot rid himself of visions of a best friend being killed.

The writing in this one is not as compelling as the message.

WHY IS THERE NO HEAVEN ON EARTH? by Ephraim Sevela, translated by Richard Lourie. New York: Harper and Row, 1982. Older-Oldest

The setting of this unforgettable novel is in pre–World War II Russia. Set in a Jewish community, the story presents scenes of family, poverty, and tragedy. An interesting juxtaposition to the story which follows.

THE WILD CHILDREN by Felice Holman. New York: Charles Scribner's Sons, 1983.

This intriguing story takes place after the Russian Revolution and during the reign of Lenin. It offers an intense view of the plight of children surviving the aftermath of war and the turmoils of political reorganization.

The "wild children," lost, abandoned, or orphaned, form groups similar to today's urban gangs. They steal food, clothing, and anything else that can help them to survive in their cave homes. The story focuses on Alex who is forced to join one of the gangs, and on his efforts to survive the process. An outstanding book!

III. VIEWS OF THE WORLD

Celebration of Life and Death

ACROSS THE CREEK by Marya Smith. New York: Little, Brown and Co., 1989. Middle-Older

Ryerson still grieves at the loss of his mother while in the midst of his stay with his maternal grandmother. Father is away seeking a place for him and his son to live. Meantime, Ryerson stays at his grandmother's farm, where there is nothing much to do except follow her to church meetings and other local activities. At the farm, there are memories of his dead mother—the places she told him about in her voice that was so soft that some could not hear her clearly. Ryerson remembers the hours of her sickness, and the days he spent sitting on her bed and listening to the stories she told. Then one day, while walking in the woods near the farm, he spots a young girl wearing a red jacket, who looks like his mother looked when she was young. Ryerson convinces himself that this is his mother, returned as a child. How could she have left him forever? When he meets the girl in the woods, her quiet withdrawn nature, and her sensitivity to him, provide more evidence that this is indeed his mother. His happiness is now found in the moments he spends with the young girl, making it easier to tolerate the demands of relating to well-intentioned but insensitive adults.

When school starts, Ryerson is in for a rude awakening. One day in the halls of the school, he meets the young girl from the woods, who is ridiculed by his new classmates and called "a retard." Dreams of the reincarnation of his mother are shattered, leaving Ryerson crestfallen. Soon his sorrow turns to guilt, because he has totally rejected the girl, and refused to acknowledge any relationship with her. He retains a nagging guilt, even after allowing his pent up grief to flow freely in tears.

When his father finds a home for the two of them in Denver,

147

Ryerson feels compelled to go once more to the meeting place in the woods and to say goodbye to the girl he found there. When they meet, he apologizes for his behavior, tells her about his grief, and gives her his very special pocket knife. The two agree never to forget each other. A poignant story about love, relationships, life, and death—with accurate portrayals of reactions to death, including anger, non-admission, and guilt.

A BEGONIA FOR MISS APPLEBAUM by Paul Zindel. New York: Harper and Row, 1989. Older-Oldest

Two young high school students write about their joyful and eventually tragic experiences with Miss Applebaum, their high school science teacher. When Miss Applebaum retires, Zela and Henry decide to visit her at her home. They find that she lives in a rather seedy apartment in New York. Her living room is cluttered with plants and/or items from old science classes. The begonia the students have brought as a gift seems like an addition to a jungle.

As the story develops, told by Henry and Zelda on the school computer, the three become a trio of friends participating in various antics. Mrs. Applebaum educates them about the history of New York which can be found in Central Park and other places. She also teaches them some pretty outrageous games like elevator roulette, and promises to show them the roller coaster in Central Park. The roller coaster turns out to be a place in the park where you can roll and coast down a hill in the grass.

Meantime the student pair have been told by Mrs. Applebaum's niece that the woman should be left alone—for she is dying of cancer. The young people decide differently and continue their visits and their antics. They also decide to intervene in Mrs. Applebaum's health care landing her reluctantly in the hospital where an operation is performed on her. Later, when Mrs. Applebaum lies dying in her apartment she asks them to bury her in the park. They put her body in a wheelchair—take it to the park and bury it.

Readers will accept many of the antics of these three, including the final burial, with disbelief. All will admit that however unlikely the events, these characters do indeed, celebrate life and death.

BLOW ME A KISS, MISS LILY by Nancy Carlstrom. Illus. by Amy Schwartz. New York: HarperCollins, 1990. Younger

Elderly Miss Lily who lives across the street, is one of Sara's best friends. They spend time together in her house and garden, and when they part, they blow kisses. Miss Lilly is kind to Sara and to others including delivering birthday wishes at the doors of neighbors. When Miss Lily gets sick and dies, Sara feels the acute pain of losing her friend. With the help of her mother and the presence of Miss Lily's cat, adopted by the family, the pain gradually diminishes. Pleasant color illustrations accompany the text.

BREADSTICKS AND BLESSING PLACES by Candy Dawson Boyd. New York: Macmillan, 1985. Middle-Older

The story begins with the ordinary struggles and events of a girl at school and at play with her friends. Toni Dawson struggles to master sixth grade math, so that she can attend King Academy the following year. The early scenarios set the stage for the deeper struggle to follow—Toni's attempt to handle grief after her friend Susan is accidently killed.

Toni's mother tries to help her deal with the loss, but Toni remains depressed and in some ways incapacitated. She is unable to improve her math, or to focus on her wish to enter King Academy.

Having experienced the loss of a family member, it is a friend, Mattie, who helps Toni. Mattie explains how she handled her own grief. After this, Toni initiates a ritual for celebrating the life and death of her friend.

THE CAR TRIP by Helen Oxenbury. Illus. by author. New York: Dial, 1983. Youngest

Children will love the humorous situations during the car trip. A realistic and jubilant portrayal of an event to which many very young children can relate.

CHICKA CHICKA BOOM BOOM by Bill Martin, Jr, and John Archambault. Illustrated by Lois Ehlert. New York: Simon and Schuster, 1989. Youngest

Adults, baby sitters, and older siblings can have a merry time sharing this rhyming, bouncing, alphabet book with pre-schoolers. The book has polka dot borders and boldly bright illustrations.

CITY SEEN FROM A TO Z by Rachel Isadora. Illus. by the author. New York: Greenwillow, 1984. Youngest

Celebrating the city, the illustrations and alphabets depict·
aspects of city life.

THE CUT-UPS by James Marshall. Illus. by the author. New York:
    Viking Kestrel, 1984. Youngest

Laughter and just plain silliness are enjoyed in this picture
story about children involved in humorous antics.

EVERETT ANDERSON'S GOODBYE by Lucille Clifton. Illus.
by Ann Grifalconi. New York: Henry Holt and Co., 1983.
Younger

Marvelous, soft, charcoal pencil illustrations accompany this
portrait of a young boy's struggle with grief after his father's death.
The author's intent was to deal with the process of grief as indicated
in the introductory page where the five stages of grief are named.

FARM ALPHABET BOOK by Jane Miller. Illus. by the author.
New York: Prentice Hall, 1984. Youngest

For children in rural areas and for those in cities to gain
information about farm life, this alphabet book shows animals and
life on the farm.

FOLLOW THE DRINKING GOURD. Story and pictures by
Jeanette Winter. New York: Alfred A. Knopf, 1988. Middle

Pictures and text celebrate the escape of slaves to freedom,
using the words of simple folk songs.

FOURS CROSSINGS by Nancy Garden. New York: Farrar,
Straus and Giroux, 1981. Middle-Older

A young girl moves to Fours Crossings after her mother's
death. As she mourns, Melissa becomes friendly with a young boy,
Jed, whose father is an alcoholic. Eventually, the two become
involved in a mystery-fantasy surrounding a set of antique plates
which control the coming of Spring. They have been stolen by a
hermit who resents the modern changes in the local spring festival
of trees, which brings the change of seasons.
    Although this is fantasy, it is locked in the symbolism of life
and death, mourning and rebirth. As the mystery of the lost spring

is resolved, the child rises from the depth of mourning, with no more dreams of her dead mother—to face her new life in a new place. The symbolism will be lost on children, but those with imagination will sense the sorrow and relief.

GOOD NIGHT, MR. TOM by Michelle Magorian. New York: HarperCollins, 1982. Middle-Older

Although this novel is set in England during World War II, it is not a story about war. Some of the situations in the story are caused by the war but primarily this is a tragic story about an abused child. When the cities of England are being bombed, many parents have sent their children to safer small country villages to live with families there. It is during this period that Willie comes to live with Mr. Tom, a lonely widower. Mr. Tom finds that Willie is frail, timid, undernourished and marked with the scars of cruel punishment.

The story then moves into the segment where Willie and Mr. Tom become a family. For the first time Willie knows what it means to be loved. He establishes friendships, learns to read, and has his first birthday party complete with sweets and presents. Life for both Willie and Mr. Tom has become more complete. Willie participates in the normal escapades of childhood and Mr. Tom becomes more a part of the community.

Readers are given their first real view of Willie's crazed and abusive mother when she sends for him to return to London. Although Willie and Tom both desperately wish for Willie to stay in the village, he must go. Swiftly, Willie is cast back into the living situation of physical and verbal abuse. In addition, his mother has had another child.

Mr. Tom senses that all is not well and goes to the city to rescue Willie. Raw scenes surrounding the rescue and Willie's condition when found, follow. The boy has been left locked in a closet with no food, no water and no heat. The baby is dead and if Tom had not arrived, Willie obviously would have suffered the same fate.

The conflict then turns to Tom's attempts to persuade the authorities to allow him to take Willie home. Because he is not a blood relative, nothing can be done legally, so he kidnaps Willie and takes him back to the village to safety, knowing the authorities will appear again someday.

When the authorities come, they allow Tom to adopt Willie. Nothing pleases Tom more than the day that Willie calls him "dad."

This touching tale celebrates humanity through the childless old man who instinctively knows how to relate to a little boy. It celebrates friendship through the relationship between Willie and the friends he finds in the little village. It celebrates life and death through the relationship between Willie and Zach, another refugee in the village. Zach dies when he returns to the city during one of the worst periods of bombing. Most of all this book celebrates love.

GRANDPA'S GREAT CITY TOUR, an Alphabet Book by James Stevenson. Illus. by the author. New York: Greenwillow, 1983. Youngest

Scenes of the city presented here are hilarious—guaranteed to provide laugh-filled moments for the young.

HAPPILY AFTER ALL, by Laura C. Stevenson. New York: Houghton Mifflin, 1990. Middle-Older

When her wealthy father dies, ten-year-old Rebecca is sent from Santa Barbara to live with her mother in Vermont. Her mother, who left her when she was two, lives on a shabby farm. The story follows Becca as she rises from her sorrow and into a new life. New friends and her need to relate to her mother are now the focus of her life.

THE HAPPY FUNERAL by Eve Bunting. Illus. by Vo Dinh Mai. New York: HarperCollins, 1982. Middle

Depicted are the customs of a Chinese American funeral when a young Chinese American girl's grandfather dies. The family observes traditional customs and remembers happy experiences.

HOLDING TOGETHER by Penelope Jones. Scarsdale, N.Y.: Bradbury Press, 1981. Middle-Older

The reactions of family members when a mother dies are portrayed. Family unity in a time of sorrow is the focus of this story.

HOW COULD YOU DO IT, DIANE? by Stella Pevsner. New York: Clarion, 1989. Older

Bethany, fourteen years old, deals with the questions, the guilt, the anger felt, and the adjustment after her stepsister has committed suicide.

LORD OF THE DANCE, AN AFRICAN RETELLING, retold by
Veronique Tadjo. Illus. by the author. Youngest-Middle

A West African artist makes her portrayal of the history, lore,
and spirit of masks, a celebration in color. Striking geometric
designs decorate the book. One person calls it a "tribute to the
Senufo people." According to the author, the book was inspired by
Sydney Carter's hymn "Lord of the Dance." The interpretation is an
African celebration of masks.

LOSING UNCLE TIM by Mary Kate Jordan. Illus. by Judith
Friedman. New York: Whitman, 1989. Younger

A compassionate story of a young boy who loses his Uncle Tim
to the disease AIDS. Uncle Tim, an antique dealer, has been a
loving companion to his nephew, when his health begins to decline.
Daniel's parents help him to understand the disease, giving him
frank information about its communicability. After his uncle's
death, Daniel finds that he is remembered in his uncle's will.

LOVING BEN by Elizabeth Laird. New York: Delacorte, 1989.
Older

Anna tells the very personal and touching story of the life and
death of her baby brother, born with hydrocephalus. Ben lives long
enough for Elizabeth to form a bond with him which will affect her
life and her relationship to other children.

M.V. SEXTON SPEAKING by Suzanne Newton. New York:
Viking, 1981. Older-Oldest

At last, a novel appears which celebrates a young girl moving
into womanhood with positive and introspective behavior. M.V.
Sexton experiences the usual adolescent qualms, but partially
because of the adults who intervene in her life, she is a likeable
heroine. M.V. has been raised by Aunt Gert and Uncle Milton, At
sixteen years of age, Aunt Gert encourages her to get a job, so
Martha Venable Sexton acquires a job at a bakery where life in its
fullness begins to unfold. On her lunch hour she meets an older
man named Gene with whom she shares her thoughts about life.
Mutual friendship and respect develops.
    The young couple who own the bakery become mentors as well
as employers. M.V., already having strong principles, gains more

self-esteem through her work at the bakery and her observation of the owners. She finds herself able to ask rigid Aunt Gert, for the first time, to share information about her mother and the circumstances of her death. What she learns helps her to understand why Aunt Gert has been difficult to communicate with. The exhilaration of M.V's awakening is contagious, inspiring Uncle Milton to come out of his shell and contact an old friend. M.V. begins to date the boy who lives across the street. When Gene, the older man, confesses his enchantment with her, M.V. is able to gently reject his advances. She is thankful to Aunt Gert for encouraging her to get a job and she is thankful for learning experiences provided for her through her work. All of these matters are written about with a sense of joyous exploration, exemplified by the hilarious scene at the bakery when the owners engage in a meringue throwing fight with their benefactor. This book is also one of the few which offers a realistic view of employment.

MIRANDY AND BROTHER WIND by Patricia C. McKissack. Illus. by Jerry Pinkney. New York: Alfred A. Knopf, 1988. Middle

This story commemorates an event in the life of the author's grandparents, inspired by a picture of them winning a cakewalk contest when they were teenagers in 1906. The story has the delightful quality of folklore with pictures which transmit the sense of the community which is the background for the story. For young readers, this is a story to experience for its pure joy. The book could be used with older readers to delve into some of the historical facts about the cakewalk, which are not all as pleasant as this story. The cakewalk can be traced from slavery to the demeaning portrayals of minstrel performers, but this book does not allow such historical facts to detract from an opportunity for celebration.

MY FAVORITE PLACE by Susan Sargent and Donna Aaron Wirt. Illus. by Allan Eitzen. New York: Abingdon Press, 1983. Younger

The joys of being at the beach are made even more exciting when the reader learns at the end that the narrator is blind.

PARADE by Donald Crews. Illus. by the author. New York: Greenwillow, 1983. Youngest

What event is more festive than a parade? Crews's illustrations provide the motion and activity for children to relive moments in a parade. Why not read this book with march music playing in the background and have the children parade afterward?

PARK'S QUEST by Katherine Paterson. New York: Dutton, 1988. Older

Parkington Waddell Broughton, the Fifth, wants to learn about his father who died in Vietnam. After a trip to the Vietnam Memorial, where he does a rubbing of his father's name, the need becomes more compelling. He confronts his mother seeking information about his father's family. Finally his mother allows him to travel to his grandfather's farm in Virginia, where a complicated story begins to unfold.

An interesting device is used by the author as Parkington speaks through fantasies of Knights of Old.

PENNIES FOR THE PIPER by Susan MacLean. New York: Farrar, Straus and Giroux, 1981. Older

A moving story of a young girl, alone, facing the death of her mother. Ten-year-old Bick shows unusual resiliency when her mother dies and she has to make the arrangements alone, and with limited funds.

QUENTIN BLAKE'S ABC by Quentin Blake. Illus by the author. New York: Alfred A. Knopf, 1989. Youngest

Cheer and humor are abundant in this alphabet book. For instance, "B is for breakfast we're having in bed," with pictures showing a mother in bed with her two children accompanied by stuffed animals. Look closely and find the cockatoo on the headboard.

RAGTIME TUMPIE by Alan Schroeder. Little, Brown and Co. (Joy Street), 1989. Illus by Bernie Fuchs. Younger-Middle

Celebrates the life and times of Josephine Baker, through a somewhat romanticized but worthy fictional account of her childhood. Children will respond to the joyful atmosphere created, festive with dance. The paintings by Bernie Fuchs are magnificent.

RED ROVER, RED ROVER by George Ella Lyon. New York: Orchard Books, 1989. Middle-Older

A story of growing up and, indeed, dealing with life and death. Sumi is moving into the difficult period of adolescence, after her grandfather has died. Her mother has retreated in her sorrow and her brother leaves for boarding school. Handling the feelings of emptiness is not easy but Sumi survives. Descriptive scenes about Sumi's starting to menstruate might be useful in discussions of sexuality.

THE REMEMBERING BOX by Eth Clifford. Illus. by Donna Diamond. New York: Houghton Mifflin, 1985. Middle

A quiet, touching story of the relationship between a boy and his grandmother ending with her death. Poignant but real.

SEAWARD by Susan Cooper. New York: Atheneum, 1983. Older

In her inimitable style, Cooper produces an allegory of life and death, using two characters who have experienced tragedy in their lives. West and Cally have entered a world of new dimensions, each from a different circumstance. The dynamics of this place are like a game of chess, which the two must understand and play in order to survive. As the strangers' lives are interwoven they are also learning that life and death are also inextricably interwoven.

SO LONG, GRANDPA by Elfie Donnelly. Translated by Anthea Bell. New York: Crown, 1981. Middle

Michael's loving relationship with his grandfather is interrupted by the fact that grandfather has cancer. As the communication between the two continues, parents and grandfather prepare Michael for his grandfather's death. The story flows quietly, easily and naturally through the illness, grandpa's death, and even the funeral at which Michael faints. A warmly reassuring ending is provided when father gives Michael a letter addressed to him by his grandfather.

SWEET CREEK HOLLER by Ruth White. New York: Farrar, Straus and Giroux, 1988. Middle-Older

This story could easily have been written as a tragic melodrama, but instead it is a tribute to human resiliency and the ability of children to find joy amid painful circumstances.

Set in the hills of Appalachia, the story spans five years in the lives of a coal mining family. the author establishes a wonderful sense of place without long descriptive passages—and the characters are very well drawn.

Virginia Carol Short and her sister Junie Marie, are aged six and seven respectively, when their father was murdered. As a result the family has to move out of the house owned by the mining company to a small rickety shack which their grandfather assists their mother in buying. The walls are thin and there is no refrigeration, but grandfather (Poppy) promises to help them.

For months, they barely survive on daddy's social security check and the girls become involved with the young people in their new community—at school and at play.

Mystery surrounds the house at the top of a hill where mining residue smolders in a black pit behind the house. Rumor has it, that the old lady who lives in the house with her son is crazed. and the myth further states that old Mr. Clancy murdered his two young daughters in that house.

The story progresses, offering the reader joyful and humorous scenes of the children at school and at play; near tragedy when Virginia becomes ill from malnutrition; friendship gone awry when Lou Jean their first and best friend becomes pregnant; the effects of gossip when rumors begin that the girls are molested by Lou Jean's father; the compelling nature of superstition when the girls believe they actually see the dead girls from the Clancy house; and finally the joys of facing a new life when Josh Clancy who has fallen in love with their mother arranges for the family to move to a new place and to start a new life. The story abounds with many wonderful scenes warmly celebrating life amid poverty while exposing the vicious effects that rumor and gossip can cause.

WHAT'S SILLY? by Niki Yektai. Illus. by Susannah Ryan. New York: Clarion, 1989. Youngest

A cartoon family goes through the day doing silly things. Pictures are shown first upside down, then right side up.

WHEN GRANDFATHER JOURNEYS INTO WINTER by Craig Kee Strete. Illustrated by Hal Frenck. New York: Greenwillow, 1979. Middle

Another special relationship between grandfather and grandson is pictured here, but this time set in American Indian culture. Grandfather makes the ultimate sacrifice for his grandson when he rides the wild black stallion to win a horse for his grandson. Tayhua has been warned by his doctors that his heart is now to weak for him to break wild horses.

When death is near, Tayhua sends for his grandson. During the bus ride home Little Thunder remembers the good times. Grandfather's words for the boy are, "The life of a man is like the life of a bird. He has a journey of spring and summer which he must travel. In this time, he builds the nest of his life and raises his young. . . . Each year they raise their families and when the winter comes each bird is on his own, each little bird must make his own journey. So it is with you, so it is with me."

WHO KILLED CHRISTOPHER? by Irina Korschunow. Translated from German by Eva L. Mazer. New York: Philomel, 1980. Older-Oldest

Who is to blame for Christopher's death? Was his death an accident or suicide? His best friend Martin remembers incidents at home, at school, and with friends which could have driven Christopher to such drastic action. In his grief and feeling his share of guilt, Martin seeks someone to blame.

WINTER HOLDING SPRING by Crescent Dragonwagon. Illus. by Ronald Himler. New York: Macmillan, 1990. Middle

Sarah's mother has died, but to this eleven-year-old child, she is still around. Everything reminds her of her mother including twirly skirts, spaghetti with basil, a sweater with cows on it, etc. Sarah's sorrow is shared by her father. Tender moments between the two are portrayed. Although this book is directed to the very young, the format seems more appropriate for older children.

PROGRAMMING SUGGESTIONS FOR SECTION III

1. To give young people an idea about other cultures invite exchange students to do a series of talks, slide shows (if they have pictures), and/or discussions based on books and films.

2. Plan your own series of library "exchange" programs, holding discussions in libraries. Exchange with schools with a different cultural base—choosing the students to participate and arranging the discussion with a librarian, teacher, or other counterpart. Public libraries and individual classes could try the same idea. Students could be required to read from a selected list of books.

3. For self-esteem and learning, ask each child to make a statement about the contributions of people represented from some part of their heritage. The statement would end with one or more things that group has contributed to the American culture. For example: "I am Chinese. Chinese people helped build America's railroads."; "I am African American, an African American named Benjamin Banneker designed the nation's capitol, Washington, D.C."; "I am Mexican American, Mexican Americans were among the first settlers of Los Angeles and other parts of the Southwest." If children are too young to seek such information on their own, teachers and librarians could write out the lines. Older children need only to be directed to the resources.

4. Hold a "SAVE THE ENVIRONMENT" or "SAVE THE PLANET WEEK," with appropriate speakers. To focus on the responsibility toward animals, contact the local pound for speakers. They could bring a few animals to schools and libraries. as examples of why pets should be cared for properly and spayed and neutered. A "Bless the Animals Day" could be held on Saint Francis of Assisi Day. To prepare for these events fiction and non-fiction on the environment could be read and discussed. Initiate your own Johnny Appleseed award, given for essays in response to literature or to children who write about their efforts to preserve the environment.

5. Find artists in the community who have examples of enviromental art, including landscape artists. Present a program featuring these artists. An "Artists in Residence" program with this purpose could be funded by grants.

6. Work out a program with the political science department at local colleges to discuss political responsibility with young people in high schools.

7. Read fiction and discuss the political systems which are/were causal to the plight of those in the stories or novels.

8. Take young people to visit the city council or other governing bodies. Try to visit at a time when issues are being discussed to which children can relate, or arrange a session with council members to discuss with children their political responsibilities.

9. Invite appropriate speakers to talk to young people about the Holocaust, after reading some of the fiction listed in the text.

10. Many Japanese are now more willing to speak about the experiences of internment during World War II. Contact Japanese organizations to find speakers.

11. Contact various veteran organizations—bring in speakers to talk about the Vietnam War and the problems suffered by veterans.

12. Hospices are a good source for speakers about life and death issues. Sometimes, youth volunteers are needed to be trained for hospice work. In every city, hospitals have children who are dying. A letter-writing program could be established after children are fully informed about the plight of these children.

SELECTED AUDIOVISUALS

1. Celebration of Life and Death
   VERY GOOD FRIENDS, 16 mm, 29 min. Color, Learning Corporation. Middle. Adaptation of Constance Greene's, BEAT THE TURTLE DRUM. Use with the book and:
   Breadsticks and Blessing Places by Dawson
   Goodnight, Mr. Tom by Magorian
   Sisters, Long Ago by Kehret
   On My Honor by Bauer

2. War and Peace—Perils of War (Rap Music)
   BOMBS AREN'T COOL. Videocassette, 59 min. With teacher's guide. Middle-Older. Use with:
   Any titles for older readers, from the section on War and Peace

3. Politics—History—Depression Years
   1929–1941: THE GREAT DEPRESSION. videocassette. Black and White. 25 min. With Teacher's Guide. National Geographic. Use with:
   Blatherskite by Potter
   The Coming Home Cafe by Pearson

4. Politics—History—Civil Rights Movement
   EYES ON THE PRIZE II-THE TIME HAS COME, 1964–
   1966. videocassette. color, 59 min. PBS Video, 1990. Middle-
   Oldest. Use with:
   Jump Ship to Freedom, Willy Freeman, Who Is Carrie? by Collier
   The Road to Memphis (and other titles by this author) by Taylor
   Tancy by Hurmence

5. Politics—Apartheid
   CHAIN OF TEARS. videocassette, color, 52 min. Older-
   Oldest. Use with:
   Beyond Safe Boundaries by Sachs

6. Politics—History—China
   CHINA MOON: THREAD OF HISTORY. videocassette,
   color. Older. Use with:
   Homesick: My Story by Fritz

7. Peace (Songs including friendship and peace)
   THE FROG'S PARTY MUSIC. 1 cassette, 40 min. A Gentle
   Wind. Youngest. Use with:
   All books for youngest-younger readers.

8. Environment
   TROUBLE IN THE FOREST. 16 mm., or videocassette.
   National Film Board of Canada. 120 min. Middle-Older. Use
   with:
   The Talking Earth by George
   On the Far Side of the Mountain by George (and other titles by
   this author)
   The Dying Sun by Blackwood

9. Religion
   CHRISTIANITY AND CIVILIZATION (set). 2 filmstrips
   with 2 cassettes, 74 frames, 12 min. each. With Teacher's Guide
   and 12 activity sheets. Middle-Older.
   Best used with non fiction titles, presenting comparative
   information about other religions. Fiction titles in the section on
   Religion and Politics could be used for follow up discussions.

10. War and Peace
    MY BROTHER'S KEEPER: THE HOLOCAUST
    THROUGH THE EYES OF AN ARTIST. filmstrip cassette,
    auto and manual. With Teacher's Guide. Middle-Oldest. Use
    with:

Number the Stars by Lowry
The Devil in Vienna by Orgel
Grace in the Wilderness by Siegal
Why Is There No Heaven on Earth by Sevela

11. War and Peace
    HISTORY OF THE WARSAW GHETTO. Middle-Oldest.
    Use with:
    The Island on Bird Street by Orlev
    (See above no. 10.)

12. Politics—Blacklist Cinema Guild
    THE DAY THE COLD WAR CAME HOME. videocassette,
    color, 21 min. Cinema Guild. Older-Oldest
    No fiction titles were found which dealt directly with the
    period and results of blacklisting. Politically, the issues were
    related to free speech and press. Could be used with:
    The Ninth Issue by Dallin

13. War and Peace
    KOREAN WAR: THE UNTOLD STORY. videocassette,
    color, 33 min., Pyramid. Older-Oldest. Use with:
    All titles in War and Peace section

14. War and Peace
    THE KOREAN WAR (series). 16 mm. or videocassette, color,
    3 films approx. 15 min. ea. With Teacher's Guide. Corinet.
    Older-Oldest

15. Politics—American Indians
    BROKEN TREATIES (American Documents Series). 16 mm.
    or videocassette. With Teacher's Guide. Older. Use with:
    When Thunders Spoke by Sneve
    Drift by Mayne
    The Talking Earth by George

16. Politics—Vietnam
    VIETNAM (The Changing Face of Communism Series).
    16mm. or videocassette, color, 25 min. With Teacher's Guide.
    Middle-Older. Use with:
    A Boat to Nowhere by Cortski
    Voyage of the Lucky Dragon by Bennett

17. Politics—Apartheid
    NELSON MANDELA, THE LONG WALK TO FREEDOM.
    videocassette, color, 28 min. Middle-Older. Use with:
    Beyond Safe Boundaries by Sachs

18. Celebration of Life and Death
    TEENAGE SUICIDE: THE ULTIMATE DROPOUT. 39
    min. PBS Older-Oldest. Use with:
    Who Killed Christopher? by Korschunow
    The Dancing Madness by Ames
    How Could You Do It, Diane? by Pevsner

19. Environment—Acid Rain
    THE ENDANGERED EARTH: THE POLITICS OF ACID
    RAIN. videocassette, color, 58 min. Films for the Humanities
    Older-Oldest. Use with:
    Drift by Mayne
    The Dying Sun by Blackwood

20. War and Peace
    IN THE EVENT OF A CATASTROPHE. videocassette, 59
    min. PBS. Oldest. Use with:
    Hairline Cracks by Taylor
    Downwind by Moeri
    Los Alamos Lights by Bogard
    My Hiroshima by Morimoto

21. Environment—Rivers
    THE RIVER FARMER. 16 mm. or videocassette. color,
    Filmmakers Library. Older-Oldest. Use with:
    Let the River Be by Cummings

22. Celebration of Life and Death (Death of a young boy's father)
    A SHOCKING ACCIDENT. 16 mm, 25 min. Direct Cinema.
    Middle-Older. Use with:
    Across the Creek by Smith
    Red Rover, Red Rover by Lynn

23. Politics—Nuclear Arms Race
    TEENAGERS AND THE NUCLEAR ARMS RACE (Soap
    Box Series). videocassette, 30 min, PBS. Older-Oldest. Use
    with:
    Children of the Dust by Lawrence

24. Politics
THE KLAN: A LEGACY OF HATE IN AMERICA. 16 mm.
30 min. Films, Inc. Older. Use with:
Circle of Fire by Hooks
Morning Glory Afternoon by Brown

25. Politics—Apartheid
BISHOP DESMOND TUTU: APARTHEID IN AFRICA
(Nobel Prize Series). videocassette, color, approx. 15 min.
With student notebook. Older. Use with:
Beyond Safe Boundaries by Sachs

26. War and Peace
VIETNAM MEMORIAL (frontline). videocassette, 52 min.
PBS. Older-Oldest. Use with:
And One for All by Nelson
December Stillness by Hahn
Long Time Passing by Jones
Pocket Change by Jensen
The Wall by Bunting
Where the Elf King Sings by Wolkoff

27. Celebration of Life and Death
DYING. videocassette, 97 min, PBS. Oldest. Use with:
A Begonia for Miss Applebaum by Zindel
Four Crossings by Gardner
Seaward by Cooper

28. Religion and Culture
ISLAM, THE VEIL AND THE FUTURE. videocassette, 29
min. Older-Oldest. Use with:
Shabanu: Daughter of the Wind by Fisher

29. Religion and Culture
HANUKKAH. videocassette, 29 min. PBS. Middle-Oldest.
Use with:
December Secrets by Giff
The Rabbi's Girls by Hurwitz
What Happened to Heather Kopkowitz by Herman

SOURCES AND NOTES

1. ADOPTION BOOKS OVER TWO DECADES by Pat Lipton Sharp. TON, Winter, 1982, vol. 38, no. 2, pp. 151-157.

   The article discusses some of the positives and negatives in books dealing with adoption, for children and adolescents. The author states that, "Most of the books on adoption over the last two decades have presented idealized accounts of stereotypical children and adolescents." (note date)

2. ADVENTURING WITH BOOKS, A BOOKLIST FOR PRE-K-GRADE 6. Prepared by the Committee on the Elementary School Booklist of the National Council of Teachers of English. Diane L. Monson, editor. Urbana Ill.: NCTE.

3. AMERICAN INDIAN STEREOTYPES IN THE WORLD OF CHILDREN: A READER AND BIBLIOGRAPHY by Arlene B. Hirschfelder. Metuchen, N.J.: Scarecrow Press, 1982.

   Bibliography is divided into Section I: Stereotyping of Native Americans; and Section II: "Corrective" Materials. (For a list of American Indian Publishers from whom materials can be purchased with accurate tribal and cultural information, write: Rosalie McKay, Native American Studies Center, University of California at Berkeley.)

4. ANTI BIAS CURRICULUM; TOOLS FOR EMPOWERING YOUNG CHILDREN by Louise Derman-Sparks and the A.B.C. Task Force, NAEYC, 1989.

   Suggests ways of overcoming bias in the curriculum, under the premise that bias hampers the development of all children. Prepared by a multiracial group of educators.

5. AIDS, a pamphlet published by the Association for Library Services to Children. Includes annotated listings of fiction and nonfiction books for young readers. Write American Library Association Graphics, 50 E. Huron Street, Chicago, Ill. 60611, for quantity prices.

6. ALTERNATIVE PRESS PUBLISHERS OF CHILDREN'S BOOKS, A DIRECTORY. Madison Wis.: Cooperative Children's Book Center: Distributed by Friends of CCBC, 1985.

7. ASSESSING MORAL STAGES: A MANUAL by Lawrence Kohlberg and others. Boston: Harvard University Center for Moral Education, 1976.

Stages of moral development in youth and how they relate to educational programs.

8. ARBUTHNOT LECTURES, 1980-1989. American Library Association Publishing Services, 50 E. Huron St., Chicago, Ill., 60611.

Contains the lectures of ten distinguished leaders in the world of children's literature including Aidan Chambers, quoted in the introduction to this volume.

9. BABYWISE, BOOKING A HEAD START FOR PARENTS by Cathleen A. Towey. In School Library Journal, Sept., 1990, vol. 36, no. 9, pp. 148-152.

Encourages reading aloud to babies and programs to assist parents in giving their babies a head start in reading.

10. THE BEST BOOKS FOR CHILDREN PRESCHOOL THROUGH GRADE 8, 4th ed. by John T. Gillespie and Corinne J. Naaden. New York: Bowker, 1990.

11. THE BLACK EXPERIENCE IN CHILDREN'S LITERATURE. New York Public Library, Office of Branches, 455 Fifth Ave, New York, N.Y. 10016.

Selected by the NYPL Black Experience in Children's Literature Committee. Includes books about and from the United States, South and Central America, The Caribbean, Africa and England.

12. BOOKALOGUES, Multicultural Children's Books by Miriam Martinez and Marcia Nash. In Language Arts Magazine, Oct., 1990, vol. 67, no. 6. Oct., 1990.

Presents questions about multicultural learning followed by book reviews. The following titles are recommended in ethnic categories:

African American:

CHITA'S CHRISTMAS TREES by Elizabeth Fitzgerald. New York: Bradbury, 1989. Ages 4-8.

TELL ME A STORY, MAMA by Angela Johnson. Illus. by David Soman. New York: Orchard Books, 1989. Ages 4-9.

RAGTIME TUMPIE by Alan Schroeder. Illus. by Bernie Fuchs. New York: Little, Brown and Co., 1989. Ages 7-11.

WILLIE'S NOT THE HUGGING KIND by Joyce Durham Barrett. Illus. by Pat Cummings. New York: HarperCollins, 1989. Ages 4-8.

THE TALKING TREE by Robert D. San Souci. Illus. by Jerry Pinkney. New York: Dial, 1989. Ages 5-10.

THE SHIMMERSHINE QUEENS by Camille Yarborough. New York: Putnam, 1989. Ages 10-up.

Anglo American-Appalachian and Ozark Mountain:

THE THREE LITTLE PIGS AND THE FOX by William H. Hooks. Illus. by S.D. Schindler. New York: Macmillan, 1989. Ages 4-12.

GOOD MORNING GRANNY ROSE by Warren Ludwig Putnam. New York: Putnam, 1990. Ages 4-10.

THE YEAR OF THE PERFECT CHRISTMAS TREE by Gloria Houston. Illus. by Barbara Cooney. New York: Dial, 1988. Ages 6-11.

NO STAR NIGHTS by Egan Smucker. Illus. by Steve Johnson, New York: Alfred A. Knopf, 1989. Ages 7-11.

Asian:

NINE IN ONE, GRRR! GRRR! by Cathy Spagnoli (Adapted). Told by Blia Ziong. Illus. by Nancy Hom. New York: Childrens Press, 1989. Ages 4-10.

ELAINE, MARY LEWIS, AND THE FROGS by Heidi Chang. New York: Crown, 1988. Ages 6-9.

Hispanic:

THE VERY FIRST THANKSGIVING, PIONEERS ON THE RIO GRANDE by Bea Bragg. Illus. by Antonio Castro. Tucson: Harbinger House, 1989. Ages 7-11.

SPANISH PIONEERS OF THE SOUTHWEST by Joan Anderson. Photographs by George Ancona. New York: Dutton (Lodestar Books), 1989.

Native American:

HOW GLOOSKAP OUTWITS THE ICE GIANTS AND OTHER TALES OF MARITIME INDIANS by Howard Noterman. Illus. by Michael McCurdy. New York: Little, Brown and Co. 1989. Ages 8-12.

LADDER TO THE SKY by Barbara Jester. Illus. by Helen K. Davie. New York: Little, Brown and Co. 1989. Ages 5-12.

BABY RATTLESNAKE by Lynn Moroney adapted and told by Teata. Illus. by Yeg Reisberg. New York: Childrens Press. 1989 Ages 4-8.

SWEET GRASS by Jan Hudson. New York: Philomel, 1989. Ages 10-up.

13. BOOK BAIT: Detailed Notes on Adult Books Popular With Young People, 4th ed. by Elinor Walker. Chicago: American Library Association, 1988.

14. BOOKLIST (Periodical). Chicago: American Library Association.

For reviews of children's books and for special lists and features on children's literature. Write to the publisher for special lists on

The Environment, May 15, '84, The Immigrant Experience, Jul., '85; Intergenerational Relationships, May 1, '80; The Nuclear Threat, Mar. 15, '84; Peace, Apr., '87; Black Americans, Feb. 1, '87; The Chinese, Feb. 1, '85; Self-Adjustment Stories, Jul., '82; and others.

15. BOOKS TO HELP CHILDREN COPE WITH SEPARATION AND LOSS, 2nd ed. by Joanne E. Bernstein. New York: Bowker, 1983.

16. BOOKTALK! 2, BOOKTALKING FOR ALL AGES AND AUDIENCES, 2nd ed. New York: Wilson, 1985.

17. THE BULLETIN OF THE CENTER FOR CHILDREN'S BOOKS. Published monthly, except August. Chicago, Ill.: University of Chicago Press.

Timely reviews of children's books. For books to use with those in this text, note titles marked, DV, for developmental values.

18. CHILDREN AND BOOKS, by Zena Sutherland and May Hill Arbuthnot, 7th ed. Glenville, Ill.: Scott Foresman, 1985.

Designed for the study of children's literature.

19. CELEBRATE THE DREAM, AN ANNOTATED BIBLIOGRAPHY OF RECOMMENDED BOOKS FOR TEENS, FICTION AND NON-FICTION. New York Public Library, Office of Branches, 455 Fifth Ave., New York, N.Y., 10016.

20. THE CHILD AS CRITIC: TEACHING LITERATURE IN ELEMENTARY SCHOOL. New York: Teacher's College, 1975.

21. CHILDREN AS READERS by John Spink. Chicago: American Library Association, 1989.

The author, from Wales, discusses the role of reading in a child's development. Includes moral, intellectual and emotional issues.

22. CHILDREN'S LITERATURE by Francelia Butler, ed. New Haven, Conn.: Yale University Press, 1990.

23. CHOOSING BOOKS FOR CHILDREN: A COMMON-SENSE GUIDE by Betsy Hearne. New York: Delacorte, 1990.

24. A COMPREHENSIVE GUIDE TO CHILDREN'S LITERATURE WITH A JEWISH THEME by Enid Davis. New York: Schocken, 1981.

25. CREATIVE USES OF CHILDREN'S LITERATURE by Mary Ann Paulin. Hamden, Conn.: LPP Publications, Shoe String Press, 1982.

730 pages of ideas, books, media, to assist those who work with children in schools and libraries.

26. DEATH AND DYING IN CHILDREN'S AND YOUNG PEOPLE'S LITERATURE: A SURVEY AND BIBLIOGRAPHY by Marian Pyles. Jefferson, N.C.: McFarland, 1990.

Includes treatment of death and dying in folklore, nursery rhymes and classics.

27. EARLY CHILDHOOD LITERATURE SHARING PROGRAMS FOR LIBRARIES by Ann Carlson. Hamden, Conn.: LPP Publications, Shoe String Press, 1985.

Using child development information, the author suggests programs for involving children from infancy to age three in literature. Includes suggestions for work with parents.

28. EARTHWATCH III ENVIRONMENTAL READER—POLLUTION, ENERGY, CONSERVATION—A TEACHER'S GUIDE. From Earthwatch III, Institute of Enviromental Studies. University of Wisconsin, Madison, 550 N. Park Street, Science Hall, Madison, Wisconsin, 53706.

29. EMIE BULLETIN, issued quarterly by The Ethnic Materials and Exchange Round Table of the American Library Association. Write ALA/EMIERT, 50 E. Huron Street, Chicago, Ill., 60611.

Members of the committee are dedicated to the multicultural provision of literature and information. Some issues of the bulletin contain useful lists of ethnic materials for children.

30. FACTS OF LOVE IN THE LIBRARY. A VIDEO TAPE. Narrated by Patty Campbell with an introduction by Dr. Ruth Westheimer. Produced by ALA Video, address above.

31. FATHERS A PRESENCE IN PICTURE BOOKS? by Warren Stewig. In Journal of Youth Services, Summer, 1988, pp. 391-395.

Do current books show fathers interacting in the home in a wide variety of roles? Do children reading these books get a vivid sense of varied positive father images? Analyzes 100 picture books. Fathers appeared in less than half the books. The author concluded that from these books children would not receive, "a strong sense of fathers in families relating to children in a variety of ways." Interesting study.

32. FUTURE TENSE: SCIENCE FICTION CONFRONTS THE NEW SCIENCE by Janice Antczak. In School Library Journal, Jan. 1990, pp. 29-32.

Technological advancements of our times and the dangers of such technology as portrayed in science fiction for the young. Problems such as genetic engineering are discussed. Nine works are cited.

33. GROWING PAINS, HELPING CHILDREN DEAL WITH EVERYDAY PROBLEMS THROUGH READING by Maureen Cuddigan and Mary Beth Hanson. Chicago: American Library Association, 1988.

Reviews of books which fit in the following categories and/or chapters: Behavior; Child Abuse and Neglect; Death and Dying; Difficult Situations; Emotions and Feelings; Family; Fears; Friendship; Hospitalization, Illness, Health care; Safety Issues; Self-

Concept/Self esteem; Dealing with Handicaps; Sexual Equality; Understanding Society.

34. HELPING CHILDREN COPE, MASTERING STRESS THROUGH BOOKS AND STORIES by Joan Fassler. Illus. by William B. Hogan. New York: Macmillan, 1978.

Discusses the uses of books with children to help them deal with stress. Sections are Death; Separation Experiences; Hospitalization and Illness, Other Potentially Stress-producing Situations. Suggests methods of using this type of material with children. Also considers which books and approaches might be disturbing to children. (note date)

35. HERITAGE: CIVILIZATION AND THE JEWS—A GUIDE FOR USE WITH CHILDREN AND TEENAGERS by Rhonna Goodman and Freda Kleinburd. In Top of the News, Fall, 1984, pp. 99-105.

Suggests ways of using the PBS television series with children. Itemizes some books and other films. Advises that those who need films for use with elementary children write to The Board of Jewish Education, 426 W. 58th St., New York, N.Y., 10019, for their catalog.

36. THE HOLOCAUST: A BIBLIOGRAPHY FOR GRADES 6-9 by Mary Ann Paulin. In Top Of the News, vol. 42, no. 3 pp. 284-287.

Very brief annotations accompany this list of titles recommended for learning about the Holocaust.

37. INTERRACIAL BOOKS FOR CHILDREN BULLETIN. Council on Interracial Books for Children, 1841 Broadway, New York, N.Y. 10023.

38. THE IMAGE OF WORK IN ADOLESCENT FICTION by Claudia Mills. In Journal of Youth Services, Fall, 1988, pp. 76-83.

A study of thirty titles for adolescents to determine what types of images of work are portrayed. Jobs held by young adult characters and others were assessed. The authors conclusion was that if these titles are representative of the larger body of adolescent literature, "authors of adolescent fiction are failing to provide a broad and realistic view of the world of work."

39. IN THE HOMES OF STRANGERS—THE WORLD WAR II EVACUATION OF BRITISH CHILDREN IN CHILDREN'S LITERATURE by Louise Sherman. In School Library Journal, vol. 35, no. 8, pp. 42-43.

The author contends that the full story of the evacuation of children during WWII is untold in the literature now available to children. The titles discussed are:

SEARCHING FOR SHONA by Margaret Anderson. New York: Alfred A. Knopf, 1978.

VISITORS FROM LONDON by Kitty Barne. New York: Dodd Mead, 1940. O.P.

CARRIE'S WAR by Nina Bawden. New York: Lippincott, 1973.

IN SPITE OF ALL TERROR by Hester Burton. New York: World, 1969. O.P.

ALL THE CHILDREN WERE SENT AWAY by Sheila Garrigue Bradbury. New York: Lippincott, 1973.

GOOD NIGHT MR. TOM by Michelle Magorian. New York: HarperCollins, 1984.

THE OTHER SIDE OF THE FAMILY by Maureen People. New York: Henry Holt and Co., 1988.

HOW'S BUSINESS by Prince Alison. New York: Four Winds, 1988.

A TIME FOR EVERYTHING by Susan Sallis. New York: HarperCollins, 1979. O.P.

WHEN THE SIRENS WAILED by Noel Streatfield. New York: Random House, 1976.

THE DOLPHINS CROSSING by Jill Paton Walsh. New York: St. Martin Press, 1967. O.P.

FIREWEED by Jill Paton Walsh. New York: Farrar, Straus and Giroux 1970.

40. HOPE AMIDST THE RUINS: NOTES TOWARD A NU-CLEAR CRITICISM OF YOUNG ADULT LITERATURE by Millicent Lenz. In Journal of Youth Services, Spring, 1988, pp. 321-328.

Discusses fiction and non-fiction which deal with the nuclear dilemma.

41. A HISPANIC HERITAGE: A GUIDE TO JUVENILE BOOKS ABOUT HISPANIC PEOPLE AND CULTURES, by Isabel Schon. Metuchen, N.J.: Scarecrow Press, 1980; SERIES II, 1985; SERIES III, 1988; SERIES IV, 1991.

42. HORN BOOK MAGAZINE. Boston: Horn Book Inc. 14 Beacon Street. Published six times a year. Now also publishing:

THE HORN BOOK GUIDE TO CHILDREN'S AND YOUNG ADULT BOOKS, "a complete comprehensive review of all hardcover books published in the previous season."

43. HOW MUCH TRUTH DO WE TELL CHILDREN, THE POLITICS OF CHILDREN'S LITERATURE edited by Betty Bacon. Minneapolis: MEP Publications, 1988.

A set of 23 challenging essays which focuses on children's literature as part of the social and political fabric of the nation and world. The essays contributed are from a wide variety of writers including the editor and Harue Palomino, retired children's librarians; Ursula Sherman, lecturer in children's literature; Mildred Walter, writer and others. Some contributions are reprints from other sources.

44. INDIAN BOOKS by Hap Gilliland. Montana Council For Indian Education, 1980.

45. JAPAN THROUGH CHILDREN'S LITERATURE: AN ANNOTATED BIBLIOGRAPHY. Compiled by Yasuko Makino, Westport Conn.: Greenwood, 1985.

46. JOURNAL OF YOUTH SERVICES (Formerly Top of the News) Chicago: American Library Association.

Directed to librarians, the journal contains articles on all aspects of serving children and youth in libraries.

47. JUNIOR FICTION: A FEMINIST CRITIQUE by Sharon Wigutoff. In Top of the News, Winter, 1982, pp. 113-124.

Examines sex role portrayals in a number of titles, and pleads for a balance in representation of women and cultural minorities in children's books.

48. LANGUAGE ARTS MAGAZINE. All Issues. National Council of Teachers of English.

Directed primarily toward teachers, but each contains some book reviews and selected issues deal with matters such as multiculturalism, families, etc.

49. LAUGHTER IN THE LIBRARY: HUMOROUS PICTURE BOOKS FOR CHILDREN by Patricia J. Wilson and Karen Kupiter. In Journal of Youth Services, Fall, 1989, vol. 3, no. 1.

Encourages adults to use books of humor with children "through which they can help youngsters develop and nourish their senses of humor." Fits well with the concept of celebration. Titles and references.

50. LEARNING ABOUT SHARING: CHILDREN'S BOOKS IN THE INTERNATIONAL SCENE, by Mildred Batchelder. In A SEA OF UPTURNED FACES: Proceedings of the Third Pacific Rim Conference on Children's Literature, ed. by Winifred Ragsdale. Metuchen, N.J.: Scarecrow Press, 1989, pp. 9-26.

51. LIBRARY SERVICE FOR FAMILIES by Marguerite Baechtold and Eleanor Ruth McKinney. Hamden, Conn.: LPP Publications, Shoe String Press, 1983.

Covers numerous aspects of library service to families including models of programs. An extensive number of materials are included for the study of the American family and for statistical information on same.

52. LIBROS EN ESPANOL PARA LOS PEQUENOS. 32 page booklet. New York Public Library, Office of Branches, 455 Fifth Ave, New York, N.Y. 10016.

Selected titles in Spanish including picture books and fairy tales. Brief annotations.

53. LITERATURE FOR THE YOUNG CHILD, 2nd. ed. by Eileen M. Burke. Newton, Mass.: Allyn and Bacon, 1990.

54. MEDUSA IN THE MALL, THE OLD MYTHS ARE PART OF THE LIVING TRADITION by Hazel Rochman. In School Library Journal, Feb., 1989, vol. 35, no. 6. pp. 30-33.

Compares the motifs of older mythological tales to the motifs in modern novels for young adults. Suggests that young adults can learn about and from these comparisons. The following titles are suggested:

THE HERO
    Cooper, *The Dark Is Rising*
    Cross, *Chartbreaker*
    Lipsyte, *One Fat Summer*
    Meltzer, *Rescue: The Story of How the Gentiles Saved Jews in the Holocaust*
    Rylant, *A Fine White Dust*
    Townsend, *The Adrian Mole Diaries*

THE MONSTER
    Alexander, *The Kestrel*
    DeJenkins, *The Honorable Prison*
    Fox, *One Eyed Cat*
    Kerr, *Gentlehands*
    McKinley, *Beauty*
    O'Neal, *In Summer Light*
    Swartout, *Bless the Beasts and Children*

PERILOUS JOURNEY
    Burnford, *The Incredible Journey*
    Cole, *The Goats*

Ehrlich, *Where It Stops Nobody Knows*
Holman, *Slake's Limbo*
Jones, *Howl's Moving Castle*
Oates, *Where Are You Going, Where Have You Been?*, in *Where Are You Going, Where Have You Been? Stories of Young America*
Voight, *Homecoming*

55. MULTICULTURAL LEARNING THROUGH CHILDREN'S LITERATURE by Timothy V. Rasinski and Nancy D. Padak. In Language Arts, Oct., 1990, vol. 67, no. 6.

"We also suggest classroom approaches that capitalize on the power of literature to promote multicultural appreciation."

56. MULTICULTURAL LITERATURE: MIRRORS AND WINDOWS ON A GLOBAL COMMUNITY by Susan Cox and Lee Galda. In The Reading Teacher, April, 1990.

57. MORE BOOK APPEAL: KEEP YOUNG TEENS IN THE LIBRARY by Karen Cornell Gomberg. Jefferson, N.C.: McFarland, 1990.

Games, fiction, crossword puzzles, fairs, field trips, etc. Many ideas suggested to keep adolescents using libraries.

58. MORE NOTES FROM A DIFFERENT DRUMMER, A GUIDE TO JUVENILE FICTION PORTRAYING THE DISABLED by Barbara H. Baskin and Karen H. Harris. New York: R.R. Bowker, 1984.

59. MULTICULTURAL LITERATURE, UPDATED VERSION OF MULTICULTURAL CHILDREN'S AND YOUNG ADULT LITERATURE, 1988. From The Cooperative Children's Book Center, University of Wisconsin, Madison. Write to CCBC Inc. P.O. Box 5288 Madison, Wisconsin, 53705.

An annotated booklist.

60. NATIONAL COMMITTEE FOR THE PREVENTION OF CHILD ABUSE (NCPCA) CATALOG. The catalog contains useful materials for parenting classes and parenting collections Write to NCPCA, 332 South Michigan Avenue, Suite 950, Chicago, Illinois, 60604-4357.

61. THE NEW REALISM COMES OF AGE by Alleen Pace Nilsen and Ken Donelson. In Journal of Youth Services, Spring, 1988, pp. 275-282.

Discusses the ways that the "problem" novel for adolescents is changing. Suggests, with examples, that todays books present a more balanced view of parents, broader, less parochial viewpoints, and more sophisticated, varied approaches to racism problems. The list of books discussed is worthy of note.

62. THE NEW REPUBLIC OF CHILDHOOD, A CRITICAL GUIDE TO CANADIAN CHILDREN'S LITERATURE IN ENGLISH by Sheila Egoff and Judith Saltman. Toronto: Oxford University Press.

Categories for reviews include: Stories of Child and Family; The Realistic Animal Story (Environmental); Native Legends.

63. NOTABLE 1989 CHILDREN'S TRADE BOOKS IN THE FIELD OF SOCIAL STUDIES. Prepared by the National Council of Social Studies, reprinted from Social Education. From: Children's Book Council, 568 Broadway, Suite 404, New York, N.Y. 10012. Send self-addressed envelope.

64. NUCLEAR AGE LITERATURE FOR YOUTH: THE QUEST FOR A LIFE-AFFIRMING ETHIC by Millicent Lenz. Chicago: American Library Association, 1990.

Analysis of books dealing with fears of nuclear war and ecological disaster.

65. ON CHILDREN AND DEATH by Elizabeth Kubler-Ross. New York: Macmillan, 1983.

66. POSITIVE ASPECTS OF THE CONTEMPORARY AMERICAN FAMILY: A LIST OF FILMS AND BOOKS. Prepared by the YASD Media Selection and Usage Committee. Introduction by Nancy Colberg, Analysis and Commentary by Louise Spain. In Top of the News, Spring, 1984, vol. 40, no. 3, pp 315-326.

Each film is briefly annotated with a group of books listed to be used with films.

67. PROMOTING WORLD UNDERSTANDING THROUGH LITERATURE, K-8 by Ester C. Jenkins. Littleton, Colo.: Libraries Unlimited, 1983.

68. PREVENTING TEENAGE SUICIDE: THE ALTERNATIVE HAND by Polly Joan. New York: Human Sciences Press, 1986.

Written by a suicide prevention specialist, this is a valuable handbook. Should be placed in parent education collections and remembered for use by all who intervene in the lives of teenagers.

69. PUBLIC BROADCAST SYSTEM (PBS) VIDEO CATALOG. Order from PBS VIDEO, 1320 Braddock Place, Alexandria, Va. 22314.

The films cover a wide breadth of subjects. For the young there is a series of films on the FEELINGS, examining anger, child abuse, divorce, love, and more.

70. READING AND RIGHTING: PAST, PRESENT, AND FUTURE OF FICTION FOR THE YOUNG. London: Collins, 1985.

71. READING FOR THE LOVE OF IT, BEST BOOKS FOR YOUNG READERS by Michele Landsberg. New York: Prentice Hall, 1987.

Over 400 books for children.

72. RECENT DETRIMENTAL AND DISTINGUISHED BOOKS ABOUT HISPANIC PEOPLE AND CULTURE. Top of the News, Fall, 1981, pp. 79-85.

73. A REFRESHING BREEZE IN YOUNG ADULT LITERATURE by Jeffrey S. Copeland. In Top of the News, Winter, 1985, pp. 147-150.

Argues against the classification of fiction into categories such as sex, family, ecology, etc. Focus should be placed on "believable characters whose beliefs, feelings, and attitudes are developed as they learn about and grow through exposure to these subjects."

74. RELIGIOUS BOOKS FOR CHILDREN by Patricia Pearl. Revised bibliography published by the Church and Synagogue Library Association for religious congregations. Nonfiction and fiction. Write CSLA, P.O. Box 19357, Portland Oregon, 97219.

75. RIF (READING IS FUNDAMENTAL) NEWSLETTER. Smithsonian Institution, Room 500, 600 Maryland Avenue, S.W., Washington, D.C., 20560.

The newsletter offers information about programs which have been used around the country to encourage reading, including parenting programs for pregnant teens. RIF Inc. also publishes several brochures which offer helpful hints for parents, teachers, and librarians. A list of such publications can be acquired from the above address.

76. REPRESENTING CHILDREN'S BOOK CHARACTERS by Mary E. Wilson. Illus. by Diane Buchanan. Metuchen, N.J.: Scarecrow Press, 1989.

Describes experiences and offers suggestions for dramatizing book characters.

77. SCHOOL LIBRARY JOURNAL, THE MAGAZINE OF CHILDREN'S YOUNG ADULT AND SCHOOL LIBRARIES. New York: Bowker.

Articles, book reviews, reviews of audio-visuals and computer software. Annual audiovisual buyers' directory.

78. SCIENCE AND TECHNOLOGY IN FACT AND FICTION, A GUIDE TO CHILDREN'S BOOKS and SCIENCE AND TECHNOLOGY IN FACT AND FICTION A GUIDE TO YOUNG ADULT BOOKS by DayAnn M. Kennedy, Stella S. Spangler, and Mary Ann Vanderwerf. New York: Bowker, 1990.

Includes science fiction with political and social implications.

79. SELECTED FILMS FOR YOUNG ADULTS—OUTSTANDING FILM AND VIDEO FOR TEENAGERS. For quantity prices contact ALSC/YALSA, American Library Association, 50

E. Huron St., Chicago, Ill. 60611. Ask for a list of other ALSC/YALSA publications.

80. SELECTED VIDEOS AND FILMS FOR YOUNG ADULTS: 1975-1985. Edited by Patsy H. Perritt and Jean T. Kreamer. Chicago: American Library Association, 1986.

A guide to use of films in programming for young adults.

81. SELECTING MATERIALS FOR AND ABOUT HISPANIC AND EAST ASIAN CHILDREN AND YOUNG PEOPLE by Patricia F. Beilke and Frank J. Sciara. Hamden, Conn.: Library Professional Publications, Shoe String Press, 1986.

Designed for librarians, this title could be helpful to teachers and others trying to include various cultures in reading lists and/or curriculum. Guidelines for avoiding cultural mistakes and stereotypes are included. Attention is paid to cultural groups, sometimes ignored, such as, Cubans and Laotians. An extensive list of references is included.

82. SEXUAL ABUSE: ITS PLACE IN CHILDREN'S FICTION by Carolyn Polese. In School Library Journal, August, 1989, vol. 35, no. 12, pp. 86-90.

Discusses the good and bad in recent books for children portraying sexual abuse.

83. SEX GUIDES· BOOKS AND FILMS ABOUT SEXUALITY FOR YOUNG ADULTS. by Patty Campbell. New York: Garland, 1987.

A must guide to a variety of resources providing sex information. Analyzes the usefulness of publications and examines audiovisuals as well.

84. SOCIETY AND CHILDREN'S LITERATURE by James H. Fraser, ed. Boston: Godine, 1978.

85. SOUTH AFRICA & APARTHEID: A MULTIMEDIA LIST FOR YOUNG ADULTS. In Booklist, November, 1984.

86. TEEN PREGNANCY CRISIS: LIBRARIES CAN HELP, A

PACKET OF HELPFUL INFORMATION. ALSC/YALSA, ALA.

87. THROUGH THE EYES OF CHILDREN, An introduction to Children's Literature. by Donna E. Norton. Columbus, Ohio: Merrill, 1983.

For the study and teaching of children's literature. Resources for teachers, helpful program and curriculum suggestions at the end of each chapter.

88. THE TREATMENT OF DEATH AND DYING IN YOUNG ADULT FICTION by Diane L. Payne. In Top of the News, Summer, 1986, pp. 375-383.

The purpose of the paper is stated as: "To explore the place of fiction in helping youth deal honestly and constructively with this 'enemy.' " "Enemy" refers to the fact that many Americans are reluctant to regard death as anything but an unnatural enemy. The discussion includes developmental understanding, reasons for using literature and the pros and cons of the literature itself. References and a bibliography of sources append the article. Books the author feels have appropriate treatments are:

Dixon, *May I Cross Your Golden River?*
  Skipper (Sequel to above)
Gerson, *Passing Through*
Little, *Home From Far*
Paterson, *Bridge to Terabitha*
Pfeffer, *About David*
Rinaldi, *Term Paper*
Scotter, *A Matter of Time*
Stolz, *The Edge of Next Year*
Winthrop, *Knock, Knock! Who's There?*

89. TRIUMPHS OF THE SPIRIT IN CHILDREN'S LITERA-TURE by Fancelia Butler and Richard Rotert, Editors. Hamden, Conn.: LPP Publications, Shoe String Press, 1986.

Twenty-five essays which are written with the assumption that literature does assist in the "triumph of the human spirit." Essays consider, fantasy, folklore, realism, and religious materials.

90. UNDERSTANDING DIVERSITY: WHAT YOUNG CHILDREN WANT AND NEED TO KNOW by Louise Derman-Sparks. In Pre-K Today. Scholastic, Nov./Dec., 1990, vol. 5, no. 3.

91. VALUES IN SELECTED CHILDREN'S BOOKS OF FICTION AND FANTASY by Carolyn Field and Jacqueline Shacter Weiss. Hamden, Conn.: LPP Publications, Shoe String Press, 1987.

92. VOICE OF YOUTH ADVOCATES (Periodical), edited by Dorothy Broderick. Metuchen, N.J., Scarecrow Press.

A *must* for those interested in materials for young adults and for those who work with young people in schools, libraries and other organizations. Reviews, feature articles, and commentary.

93. WE ARE FAMILIES by Ellen Booth Church. In Pre-K Today, Scholastic, Nov./Dec., 1990, vol. 5, no. 3, pp. 37-39.

Suggestions for affirming and learning about family in the early childhood classroom. Suggestions will help avoid ignoring or being biased to one type of family. Suggestions include: In circle time, define family by things they do together rather than what they are and who they are; Post magazine photos of families from all races and in many configurations; Discuss how families change, grow or decrease; Allow the subject of families to come up and take time for impromptu discussion; Show support for all families; and Adopt an infant—invite one of the children's parents or relatives with a baby to visit once a month or more so that the children can watch the baby grow.

94. THE WISH LIST FOR PEACE, WORLD INFORMATION SHAPES HARMONY, By the Hammond Indiana Public Library and the Gary Chapter of Women's Action for Nuclear Disarmament (WAND). An eight-page bibliography including materials for preschool-high school. Send a self addressed envelope and postage to Hammond Public Library, 564 State St. Hammond, Indiana, 46320.

95. WITNESS TO WAR: A THEMATIC GUIDE TO YOUNG ADULT LITERATURE ON WORLD WAR II, 1965-1981 by Cathryn J. Wellner. Metuchen, N.J.: Scarecrow Press, 1982.

Reviews 178 novels and memoirs. Appended references and information. Excellent for curriculum and individual use.

96. WRITERS FOR CHILDREN: CRITICAL STUDIES OF MAJOR AUTHORS SINCE THE SEVENTEENTH CENTURY. ed. by Jane M. Bingman. New York: Scribner, 1987.

97. YOUNG AND BLACK: THE BLACK EXPERIENCE IN CHILDREN'S BOOKS. Los Angeles Public Library. Children's Services, LAPL 630 W. 5th Street, Los Angeles, Ca. 90071. Lists of books for children included here as an example of beautiful packaging and cooperative programming. The illustrations are block prints provided through a cooperative arrangement with GOCART (Gallery of Children's Art) an outreach program of the Watts Towers Art Center, supervised by John Outterbridge, a well-known Black artist.

98. YOUTH INDICATORS, 1988 TRENDS IN THE WELL BEING OF YOUTH STUDY From the Government Printing Office, Washington, D.C. 20402.

Demographics, family income, education, youth employment, figures, health, behavior, and attitudes.

AUTHOR INDEX

TITLE INDEX

ILLUSTRATOR INDEX

198

O'Brien, Anne Sibley   *Jamaica's Find*
Osborn, Lois   *My Dad Is Really Something*
Owens, Gail   *The Cybil War*
Oxenbury, Helen   *The Birthday Party; The Car Trip*

Palmer, Heidi   *I Have Two Families*
Parker, Robert Andrew   *Seal Child*
Pinkney, Jerry   *Mirandy and Brother Wind*

Robinson, Charles   *The Boy Who Wanted a Family*
Rockwell, Anne   *Willy Can Count*
Rubin, Leonard   *R-T, Margaret, and the Rats of NIMH; The Runner*
Ryan, Susannah   *What's Silly?*

Simont, Marc   *If You Listen*
Sims, Blanche   *December Secrets*
Soman, David   *When I Am Old with You*
Spence, Jim   *Say Cheese*
Steptoe, John   *Daddy Is a Monster . . . Sometimes*
Stevenson, James   *I Know a Lady*
Stoke, Dorothea   *Jacob and Owl: A Story*
Stoke, Frank   *Jacob and Owl: A Story*
Strauss, Linda   *The Downtown Day*

Tadjo, Veronique   *Lord of the Dance, an African Retelling*
Tang, You-shan   *Pie-Biter*
Teicher, Dick   *A Boat to Nowhere*
Tomei, Lorna   *What Do You Do When Your Mouth Won't Open?*
Tomes, Margot   *Homesick: My Story*
Trivas, Irene   *I'm Calling Molly*

van Don, Pham   *Tuan*
Vigna, Judith   *I Wish Daddy Didn't Drink So Much*
Vivas, Julie   *The Very Best of Friends*

Weiss, Nicki   *Waiting*
Wentworth, Jane   *Cady*
Wildsmith, Brian   *Noah's Spaceship*
Wilson, Janet   *Daniel's Dog*
Winter, Jeanette   *Follow the Drinking Gourd*

Yabuuchi, Masayuki   *Animal Mothers*

ABOUT THE AUTHOR

Based in Los Angeles, California, Binnie Tate Wilkin is a consultant in library services, with concentration on public libraries and services to children. Ms. Wilkin has been a school librarian, a children's librarian and a specialist in children's services for a federally funded outreach project which brought her national recognition. Serving as Minority Services Coordinator for the Los Angeles County Public Library, she designed services for the major minority populations in Los Angeles County.

Ms. Wilkin has taught in Library Schools at the University of Wisconsin-Milwaukee, the University of California at Berkeley and the University of California at Los Angeles. Most recently, she taught and led workshops in the Children's Literature Institute at Columbia University's School of Library Service. The first edition of *Survival Themes in Fiction for Children and Young People* was published by Scarecrow Press in 1978.